T4-ACU-664

WITHDRAWN

Do we really need libraries?

Do we really need libraries?

*An assessment of approaches to the evaluation
of the performance of libraries*

JOHN BLAGDEN
Cranfield Institute of Technology

K · G · Saur   Clive Bingley

New York · London · München · Paris

First published 1980
by Clive Bingley Ltd, a member of
the K G Saur International Publishing Group
Copyright © John Blagden
All rights reserved.
Set in 11 on 12 Baskerville by CIT Press.
Printed and bound in the UK by
Redwood Burn Ltd of Trowbridge
Bingley (UK) ISBN: 0-85157-308-8
Saur (USA) ISBN: 0-89664-442-1

British Library Cataloguing in Publication Data

Blagden, John Frederick
    Do we really need libraries?
    1. Libraries — Evaluation
    I. Title
    021'.001'8   Z678.85

    ISBN 0-85157-308-8

CONTENTS

	Introduction	7
	Acknowledgements	11
1	The Purpose of Evaluation	13
2	The Methodological Problem	31
3	Some Evaluative Techniques	37
4	Approaches to Library Performance Assessment	47
5	A Review of Some Major Studies	61
6	Assessing a Construction Design Library by Market Penetration and Impact Criteria	91
7	Assessing a Management Library by Market Penetration and Impact Criteria	111
8	Performance Assessment — Where Do We Go From Here?	141
	Bibliography	147
	Index	159

INTRODUCTION

WHEN YOU tell people that you are a librarian, and you only of course confess this to the very persistent, the best reaction that you can hope for is that you don't look like a librarian. I often wonder what a brain surgeon would feel like if this was the constant reaction that he received when confessing his occupation. There is also a confusion in the world outside as to what the role of a library actually is and this of course reinforces the mystery surrounding the librarian's job.

In my view, much of this confusion has been caused by the failure of the library profession to vigorously demonstrate the part that libraries and librarians play in enriching the minds of women and men. Paradoxically this has not been helped by an attitude that is still with us, that reading is a superior way of transferring information and knowledge. This attitude would perhaps be more defensible if those taking that view would actually attempt to gather evidence to support that assumption. A theme of this book then is the search for evidence, or perhaps more specifically, for a knowledge utilization strategy of the kind promoted by McLuhan whereby the transfer of knowledge through publications is seen as complementary to, and not competitive with, other forms of knowledge transfer. It is then that one can begin to regard *some* reading as the superior way of transferring *some* knowledge.

Thus this book is a review of the attempts that have been made to develop a methodology by which a library's (and by inference the librarian's) contribution to the goals laid down by the funding body can be more easily assessed. It also examines in some detail the techniques that appear to be appropriate to this somewhat daunting task. As the book is concerned with corporate contribution, it does not concern itself with the inputs to the library system, but emphasizes the interactions between the library and the customers that it is aiming to serve. It is not a review of user studies however, but does review those studies and approaches which appear to give the library manager some clues as to how to justify the investment in the library. It focuses then on the potential benefits and disbenefits that a library may confer on a particular audience, without necessarily considering the costs of supply which although important, are relatively simple to establish.

The first half of this book, ie, up to and including chapter five is a review of approaches and problems associated with library performance assessment and is therefore essentially derivative in its nature. In the text much use has been made of quotations as I believe that more justice is done to authors by letting them speak as much as possible for themselves rather than précising and paraphrasing their arguments. Of course argument by quotation is open to serious abuse in so far as one can foist virtually any opinion on to anyone by simply quoting out of context. I hope that I have avoided this but in any case I trust that the reader who finds any of the statements that I have quoted of interest, will refer to the original author's writings. I owe a debt therefore to all the authors cited in this publication because without their help this publication would never have materialised. I would, however, single out three key titles, all of which are highly relevant to the performance assessment area namely Bryan Vickery's *information systems,* Wilf Lancaster's *the measurement and evaluation of library services* and King and Bryants *the evaluation of information services and products.*

Chapter one discusses the purpose and conceptual basis for evaluation. Chapter two briefly discusses the overall methodological problem that arise out of Chapter one. Chapter three reviews some of the key techniques that appear relevant to performance assessment studies. (This is taken very much from the viewpoint of a practitioner look however and any reader considering utilizing the reviewed techniques would be well advised to consult the more extensive publications available on research methodology. For those new to the field, Maurice Line's dated, but very readable, Library Surveys is an excellent introduction). Chapter four highlights some of the evaluative approaches that have attracted most attention and Chapter five reviews the major empirical investigations in the field. Chapter six describes the attempt to develop a new approach to performance assessment at the Greater London Council; and Chapter seven describes a more ambitious but similar attempt at the British Institute of Management. The final Chapter presents the conclusion and some thoughts for the future.

This book therefore provides a means of approaching the whole area of library performance assessment and is aimed at all those, like myself, who would like some reasonably objective answers to the question posed in the title of this book.

This book is based on a search of Library and Information Science Abstracts (1970 to date) and the Cuadra (subsequently Williams 1977) Annual Reviews of Information Science. I have also consulted bibliographies and literature reviews by Atkin, Brophy, the Bureau of Applied Social Research (some attribute this to H Menzel), Coover, Evans et al, Fabisoff & Ely, Ford (1973 and 1977) Havelock[1], Hills, Holmes, Hunter, Krevitt and Griffith, McCafferty, Moore, Noble and Ward, Olsen, Reynolds, Rodwell, Short, Waldhart and Waldhart, Wessel and Cohressen, and Wood. The Index to Library and Information Theses prepared by P J Taylor has been checked as well as the post-1974 issues of the Radials Bulletin which update the Taylor publication.

All references in the text are cited in alphabetical order of author's surname at the end of this publication. Where more than one citation from an author appears in the text, these are distinguished by the date of publication being included in brackets after the author's surname.

---

[1] Only post 1972 entries were checked because of the unhelpful alphabetical arrangement.

ACKNOWLEDGEMENTS

THE AUTHOR wishes to thank the following for permission to reproduce copyright material.

Professor T Allen and the Massachussetts Institute of Technology for extracts from *Managing the flow of technology*.

Aslib for the diagram taken from Orr's *Journal of documentation* article.

City University for extracts from the Hannah and Elwen theses.

Jane Goodey and Kate Mathew and the University of York for extracts from *Architects and information*.

R W Hall for extracts from *An investigation into the information seeking habits of scientists and engineers in industry*.

R G Havelock and University of Michigan for extracts from Bibliography on *Knowledge utilization and dissemination*.

Professor W Lancaster and Information Resources Press for extracts from *The measurement and evaluation of library services*.

Dr Christine Oldman and Cranfield Institute of Technology for extracts from her thesis.

Professor B C Vickery and Butterworths for extracts from *Information systems*.

Professor J N Wolfe and Praeger Publishers for extracts from *Economics of technical information systems*.

In addition, I would as well like to thank:

Professor B Vickery of University College for his intelligent, kind and patient supervision of the original thesis on which this book is based;

Geoffrey Ford of Southampton University and Dr Christine Oldman of Leeds University for help in clarifying my early thoughts;

The staffs of the British Institute of Management's Management Information Centre especially Gillian Dare, and the Greater London Councils Access service especially Margaret Palmer for help with the fieldwork;

Dr Jim Rose and David Hogan of the Greater London Council Behavioural Sciences Unit;

John Wilson and Hano Johannsen of the British Institute of Management;

B C Brookes of University College and Dr S Robertson of City University for their suggestions on the market penetration calculations;

David Preston of the Cranfield Institute of Technology's library service and Jack Winkler and Phil Topping of the Cranfield Social Policy Unit for reading the final draft;

Beryl Hughes and Norah Wilton for help in typing the manuscript;

And finally the staffs of the libraries of Aslib and the Library Association.

ONE

THE PURPOSE OF EVALUATION

THE MANAGEMENT process essentially consists of setting objectives, evaluating alternative ways of reaching those objectives, selecting one alternative and then monitoring the success of the selected alternative in making progress towards that objective. Monitoring or evaluation is then an integral part of the management process simply and obviously because all libraries either implicitly or explicitly (as at Kingston upon Hull public libraries) are attempting to achieve something.

Unless, therefore the library manager is able to demonstrate that some progress has been made in achieving the objectives that inspired the initial decision to invest in that library, the whole validity of that decision will be constantly under attack.

Although therefore the purpose of evaluation is clear, the timing of and the means by which such an evaluation can be accomplished is less so. For example Guba and Stufflebeam point out that evaluation often cannot take place until a particular programme has been completed. Thus feedback leading to a refinement of a current programme is lost This problem can be exacerbated in long life programmes, for example at what point does one attempt to evaluate the effectiveness of the design process in a housebuilding programme, especially where the investment in design and construction is deliberately restricted by central government, possibly at the expense of the life of that dwelling. It is difficult therefore to conduct evaluation not only because of the unique nature of many programmes and the time scale; but also because as Hamilton has rightly asserted, "no one has demonstrated how rational evaluation fits into the value laden structure of practical decision making".

The programme may be unique, long term and highly political, but an added complication for librarians is as the Bureau of Applied Research indicates.

"Whilst use of a channel can be recorded fairly easily the function served by the communication act is not easily recorded and some significant effects take place a considerable while after the receipt of a message".

King and Palmour describe an optimal library system as one "which would permit every message to be transmitted only to the recipients who will use the information, when the information is required at a cost that is less than or equal to the value of information". This statement suggests the evaluative rationale that lies behind library performance assessment, in that what is required is a *method* which will indicate how far a particular library is falling short of the King and Palmour ideal. The word method is emphasized here because what one wants to get away from is the reliance on the haphazard recording of single events that appear to justify the existence of a library.

James Ensor, sometime ago produced a whole host of examples of such events ostensibly demonstrating the severe cost penalties involved if one does not have effective access to information. A few examples from Ensor will suffice to give you a flavour of the anecdotal type justification for investing in a library. "The General Electric Company spent two years researching rain-making with dry ice and silver iodide crystals. At the end of that time they discovered that a Dutch company had published almost identical research results twenty years earlier. Research on the American space programme produced a new fluid density measurement employing the Clausius Mosotti relationship and yet, this had already been discovered 100 years ago. What was more alarming in this case was that two other centres engaged in space research had also 'invented' this process. Again in the American space programme, this time in the Apollo Manned Space Project, a contractor used methanol to pressure test twenty 100,000 dollar titanium fuel tanks for the spacecraft. Methanol was chosen because its characteristics are similar to those of the fuels which were to be used in the manned flight. After eighteen tanks had passed the 48 hour trial, the last two failed. Frantic double checks by the contractor's research staff. revealed that methanol causes stress corrosion in titanium and this was reported in the literature in 1956. Cost: 1½ million dollars". However these examples fail to convince on at least three counts:

1 no information is given as to whether a literature search was conducted prior to these expensive 'information failures' ie would libraries have actually produced the information when it was required or did they also actually fail at the time.

2 even if these information systems had been successful (and it is difficult to check on this after the event) what would the cost have been? Significantly here, Ensor maintains that a fifth of the total spending on all scientific research is directed towards collecting and disseminating information.

3 even discounting the reservations cited above, the Ensor examples still do not necessarily justify the investment of more money into libraries and other information transfer systems. The root cause of information failures in general (rather than the more exotic examples previously quoted) may well be that those practising (in whatever sphere) lack the basic knowledge to do their jobs effectively.

A good and possibly more typical example of information failure is the construction industry. According to the New Scientist an 'estimated' fifth of the United Kingdom's current £3.5 billion maintenance bill is due to the failure to apply existing *well known* basic knowledge. No library system can ever cope with fundamental educational deficiencies on that kind of scale. It may be therefore that the answer lies in the approach adopted by Munday of offering an integrated course for potential construction professionals throughout which the importance of information is stressed. Even here however it is equally important to ensure that the students do end up with the basic knowledge which the industry requires.

King and Palmour assert that generally "the ultimate value of any information communication system should be thought of in terms of the uses that are made of the information and the subsequent impact of users' scientific and technical activities. The way in which information effects the conduct of these activities is probably the most important function of a system. Obviously the knowledge gained from information and the consequent user behaviour can enhance decision making, improve an experiment, result in better research findings, reduce duplication of research, save time in the research processes and so on. Although this is the critical function of user behaviour it is rarely measured, let alone considered, in many user studies."

This has to be contrasted with those whom Hatt describes as terminal readers, ie those who are not searching for books as a means to an end but as an end in themselves. However the concept of a terminal reader is one I find difficult to comprehend in that reading to me is always a means to an end, even if that end is pure recreational escapism. Certainly special and university libraries do not set out to cater for terminal readers, although a library may unwittingly provide books and information that lead nowhere. One of the key questions here is how far can a librarian influence this situation. Terminal reading, even in the context of the public library, is queried by both Bommer, who argues for the development of measures that will compare the value of a public library's output with such competing programmes as law enforcement, refuse collection etc; and Goddard who argues that only reading that is likely to yield social benefits should be supported by public money.

Evaluation of the library system as a whole then must be concerned with how much good a library service achieves, rather than how good the library *is,* a distinction made by Orr (1973) and illustrated below.

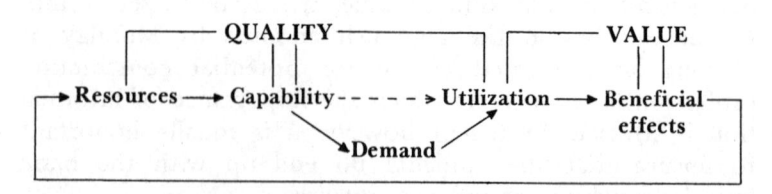

```
        ┌─── QUALITY ───┐     ┌── VALUE
        │       │       │     │   │
 ┌─→ Resources ─→ Capability ----→ Utilization ─→ Beneficial ─┐
 │                         ↘    ↗                   effects
 │                          Demand
```

This is a similar distinction to that made by Stecher when she raises two evaluative issues: "would the funds spent on the library be better spent elsewhere and are the funds allocated to the library spent in the most effective manner". It is interesting to note here that Peter Drucker maintains that the primary difference between a service institution like a library and a business is that the business receives resources by satisfying the customer, and the service institution is supported by a budget allocation from a funding source. Because the funding source and the user of the organization's products and services are separated, Drucker contends that the budget allocation for a service institution has little direct relationship to the degree of satisfaction the patron receives from the institution. Drucker observes that being paid out of a budget allocation changes what is meant by performance or results. Results in the budget-based institution means a larger budget. Performance is the ability to maintain or increase one's budget.

Inevitably then evaluation should focus on the impact that reading makes on the user, as this appears to be the most direct route for establishing how much good a library actually achieves. This is in sharp contrast to the practice described by Hatt that "at the point where the reader and book come together the librarian leaves the happy pair and tiptoes quietly away".

This traditional approach is the opposite of the approach espoused by Armstrong who argues that in the case of the farmer who borrows books on house construction, the house built is the real product. Lancaster (1977) however finds this approach completely unacceptable.

"The library has served its function adequately if it has a supply of good, readable, up-to-date books on how to construct a house and can make those available at the time the user needs them. Whether or not the reader does construct the house is governed by a myriad of factors that are completely beyond the control of the library. Moreover, of all these factors, the availability of suitable reading materials is likely to be one of comparatively minor importance. Assume, for example, that user A and user B come to a library seeking books on house construction. Both borrow materials that they consider suitable for their present purposes. A subsequently builds a house, B does not. It is doubtful that anyone could say that the library succeeded in the first case and failed in the second. It could, however, be legitimately claimed a failure if user B was unable to find suitable materials in the library at the time he needed them. The attitude adopted in this book is that a library can only be evaluated in terms of whether or not it is able to provide the materials sought by users at the time they are needed. What the user subsequently does with these materials is completely outside the librarian's control (and, some users might say, none of the librarian's business)."

But this ignores the fact that the initial decision to invest in a library is obviously based on the premise that some benefits will result and that therefore to monitor the performance of a library, some attempt should be made to discover how beneficial the library actually is. Certainly in the special library environment, the whole point of the library is to ensure some favourable outcome of the kind described by King and Palmour.

However, McLellan, a prominent *public* librarian, also supports Armstrong:

"Surely it is from the use of books from the activity of reading, that emerges the values which underlie the whole of library activity. All the books in the world produce only a negative value if there were no reading of them, if no use were made of them. What happens when a person reads? What effects does a particular book have on a variety of readers? Are they predictable effects?"

Now of course Lancaster is correct in that there are many factors which will affect the beneficial/disbeneficial impact of a book and in the final analysis this surely is the key performance indicator. The effects area in the Havelock illustration are limited and what is required here is a typology of impacts. A useful starting point is the eleven exit patterns that Hatt has identified, resulting from the reading act and apparently that is only a sample of the range of impacts that a 'message' can have on the recipient, but as Vickery (1973) states "information may be quite clearly defined as something that when acquired by a human being, causes some modification to his mind. The concept is quite clearly of significance in information systems ... But is the definition operational? By what operations can we identify modifications in the human mind?"

Let us now examine the three approaches to information system evaluation again suggested by Vickery (1973):

Dissemination and Utilization Viewed as a Process

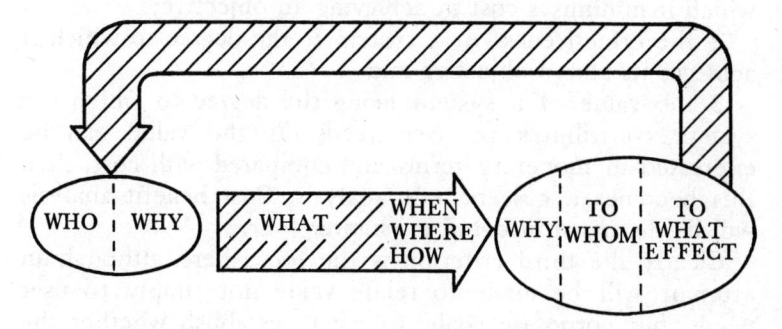

```
WHO | WHY    WHAT    WHEN      WHY | TO    | TO
                     WHERE         | WHOM  | WHAT
                     HOW                     EFFECT
```

WHO: Communicator
  Speaker
  Initiator
  Sender

WHERE: Setting
  Context
  Geographic Location
  Area
  Distance

TO
WHOM: Receiver
  Listener
  Audience

HOW: Mechanisms
  Strategies
  Ways
  Means
  Methods — Informal
  Channels — Contacts
  Medium — Conferences
           Courses
           Workshops
           Seminars
           Publications
           Mass Media

WHAT: Knowledge
  New Knowledge
  Research
  Scientific Research
  Scientific Knowledge
  Products
  Information
  Innovations
  Practices
  New Practices
  Data

FIELDS: Education
  Medicine
  Public Health
  Mental Health
  Technology
  Agriculture
  Law
  Social Welfare
  etc.

WHEN: Timing
  Stages
  Phase
  Duration
  How Long
  How Long Ago
  Sequence

WHY: Motivation
  Drive
  Resistance
  Interest
  Initiative
  Need

TO WHAT EFFECT: Result
  Criterion
  Dependent Variable
  Improvement
  Success-Failure
  Effectiveness
  Feedback

1 the economic efficiency of a system, ie the degree to which it minimises cost in achieving an objective;
2 the effectiveness of a system ie the degree to which it achieves its stated objective and
3 the value of a system being the degree to which the system contributes to user needs. If the value can be expressed in monetary terms and compared with cost, then this becomes a cost benefit analysis. Cost benefit analysis will be discussed in detail in chapter four.

Clearly the third criterion is the focus here, although an attempt will be made to relate value not simply to user needs, but corporate goals, to try to establish whether the two are necessarily entirely in harmony. This is a distinction that should be emphasized in that all library use is not necessarily of value to the user, but that use which is of value to the user, is not necessarily of value to the host organization in which the library operates. If one examines aggregated user data where the high performers have been isolated the differences in user patterns are not particularly significant as the tables from R W Hall (1969) and Tom Allen (1977) demonstrate.

Table 1 Hours per week spent by different groups reading six types of literature

	Top Performers	Technological Gatekeepers	ARAC[1] Users	Control Group
Science journals	1.60	1.83	2.59	2.11
Trade journals	2.48	2.55	2.27	2.34
Company reports	2.42	2.01	1.63	1.55
Newspapers	4.76	4.66	4.73	4.73
Engineering catalogues	.56	1.40	1.65	1.38
Sales literature	.85	1.65	1.09	1.13
Total	12.67	14.10	13.96	13.24

R W Hall (1969)

[1] Users of a specially designed information service relevant to the area studied by Hall.

These tables appear to indicate that there is no correlation between amount of use of published information and performance. The inference therefore is the somewhat unsurprising one that good technologists use information effectively.

The neglect of value, ie criteria three on the Vickery list,

Table 2 Comparison of Time Allocation Among Four Activities by Higher and Lower-Rated Project Teams

	Percent of Total Time Allocated		
	Total for Twelve Development Projects	Four Higher-Rated Projects	Four Lower-Rated Projects
Analysis and experimentation	77.3	77.9	71.4
Literature use	7.9	5.0	5.3
All communication (including literature)	16.4	13.9	13.4
Other activity	6.3	8.2	15.7
Total time reported (man-hours)	20,185	6,566	7,975

Allen 1977

has not only been because of the methodological difficulties touched on earlier but also because of a confusion (or disagreement cf Lancaster) over the purpose of a library. The recent decline in real terms of local government expenditure on public libraries for example may be due to this confusion over the purpose of a library, analgous perhaps to the reasons that Leavitt identified for the decline of the US railroads:

"every major industry was once a growth industry but some are now riding away with growth enthusiasm and others are very much in the shadow of decline. Others which are thought of as season growth industries have actually stopped growing. In every case the reason growth is threatened, slowed or stopped, is not because the market is saturated; it is because there has been failure of management. The failure is at the top. The executives responsible in the last analysis are those who deal with broad aims and policies. Thus, the railroads did not stop growing because the need for passenger and freight transportation declined. That grew. The railroads are in trouble today not because the need was filled by others (cars, trucks, aeroplanes, even telephones) but because it was not filled by the railroads themselves. They let others take customers away from them because they assumed to be in the railroad business rather than in the transportation business. The reason they defined their industry wrongly was because they were railroad-orientated instead of transportation-orientated; they were product-orientated instead of customer-orientated."

As Vickery (1973) more succinctly puts it "the overall objective of designing a system is to decide on the *output* (my emphasis) services to be provided and on the inputs from which they will be derived." Ideally it would be preferable however if one could design an information system in terms of *outcomes* likely to be achieved by certain outputs which in turn would be derived from certain inputs.

Samuelson (quoted in Vickery 1973) lists the following criteria by which a systems performance can be judged:
1 flexibility/modifiability
2 reliability (of components)
3 accessibility (of service points)
4 availability (of ultimate information)
5 response time
6 priority (queues)
7 precision (exclusion of unwanted information)
8 timeliness (currency of contents)
9 recall (of all relevant information)
10 pricing.

Lancaster (1971) has also identified the additional effectiveness criteria of coverage and amount of effort required from the user. The problem here is that these criteria are effectiveness criteria and do not provide a means by which the value of the system can be established in meeting user needs/corporate goals. Clearly, however, the system is unlikely to be a valuable system if performance effectiveness is poor.

In attempting to develop a methodology for assessing the value of a library one first has to describe the present situation, for example one would wish to establish from where do users obtain their information and what contribution does the information make towards the task or goals that they are trying to achieve. Library information must be described within the context of the total information universe to which the user is exposed. When the information inputs/outputs have been fully described we then need to conduct an analysis so that in McLuhan's words we can orchestrate the multitude of media available into a successful utilization strategy. Thus we must understand the cause and process of media effectiveness, know the strengths of each medium, so that we can assign the various channels of communication to mutually supportive roles.

Many publications distributed by libraries will be gathered to support some other activity, ie making a decision, conducting an experiment, writing a thesis etc. In order to evaluate the utility of the supplied information it will be necessary to examine the quality of the thesis, the decision and the experiment. My starting point here would be that one needs to isolate what impact (if any) the supplied information has on the decisions etc, because you can obtain good decisions despite bad information and vice versa.

Overall one would expect however there to be some correlation between the quality of supplied information and the quality of decisions taken. At some point therefore an evaluation of decisions taken will be embarked upon in a library performance assessment investigation. However as Aguilar states the "determination of whether a decision is 'correct' is not easy even after the fact. Decisions must be based on the expected outcome of future events, and the actual occurrence of an unexpected outcome does not mean that the earlier assessment was ill-judged. This is true whether results turn out much more or much less favourable than expected. In other words, a successful outcome is not proof of a wise decision, nor is an unsuccessful outcome proof of a poor decision.

Furthermore, the passage of time diminishes the possibility of determining just what did take place in the decision-making effort. Thus, an important preliminary step to this procedure would be to document the decision-making process in detail *at the time* the decision is being made, in anticipation of its eventual review. But what complications might be expected from such a procedure? Will not executives tend to hedge the record with qualifications? Will the threat of review cause executives to make more conservative decisions — a change which may be far from desirable?

Closely related is the danger that the performance appraisals may become or may be perceived as 'witch hunts'. The difficulty of convincing everyone that the purpose of an appraisal review is *to learn* and *not to cast blame* may well be the biggest stumbling block to successful adoption of this procedure."

Corporate objectives in turn can prove a complex framework against which decisions can be judged as Fred Catherwood asserts "the old axiom was business had to maximise its profits but it should exploit the market, and pay the minimum possible price for supplies and labour regardless of the social consequences. The big business today has gone a long way beyond those crude and now unworkable rules. Big business operates to a long time span. Decisions made today will pay off only in three or four years time." Many libraries of course will be funded by non profit making organizations but nevertheless decisions again will have to be evaluated over a long timespan. In addition as Burr has indicated organizations like individuals are multi goal directed which further complicates the evaluative process. In the construction environment, for example, a local authority may wish quickly to produce low cost houses, which are safe, aesthetically pleasing to the tenant and the environment, easy to maintain, functionally effective, and accessible to public transport. Clearly in evaluating the effectiveness of a design decision, and the information inputs to that decision, these often conflicting objectives will have to be weighted in order to arrive at an equitable evaluation.

In assessing the overall performance of a library there would appear to be two basic approaches (a) from the viewpoint of the user, ie, how effective is he, how he spends his time, what is the relationship between information inputs and effective performance (assuming of course that the information input can be isolated) and (b) from the viewpoint of the library manager, ie, what proportion of users were reached, what proportion of documentation borrowed was read, what proportion enriched the thinking of that individual, and did this enrichment lead to any contribution to organisational effectiveness.

Whichever approach is adopted there are three key elements involved in the evaluation: the user, the information use, and the library itself. Before proceeding further let us examine these three elements in slightly greater detail.

The user
In describing users, it is preferable to take a marketing viewpoint and define them as the total audience (market) that the library is attempting to serve. In defining that audience the market needs to be segmented because as Kuehl points out "user audiences who in total may exhibit heterogeneous use patterns and utility preferences must be classified and clustered into relatively homogeneous use segments, if the marketing concept is to be operationalised". This point is underlined by Silvey in the broadcasting context when he states "in so far as the size of the audience is a measure of a broadcast's success, it is not its absolute size that matters, but how nearly its size approaches the targets aimed at". The idea that all markets can be segmented has now received almost as widespread acceptance as the marketing concept itself.

Although the concept of segmentation is accepted there are of course many different criteria that can be employed to segment a particular target audience. Marketing has traditionally segmented markets on either a geographic basis or by employing various demographic characteristics such as age, sex or income, but in both cases product marketing analysts have found that these are generally poor predictors of consumer behaviour.

More recently a third type of segmentation has come into increasing favour, namely volume segmentation. This so called heavy half theory, according to Twedt, points out that the normal Pareto distribution applies, ie that a relatively small number of consumers account for 80% of the consumption. Therefore the effort should go into reaching the high volume consumers as they account for most of the use/consumption. The same Pareto type distribution applies to library usage patterns, but the marketing analogy falls down here, because the marketing goal of increased consumption is not the goal of most libraries in that we should be concerned with maximising beneficial usage.

However Kranzberg maintains that librarians should adopt the Twedt basis for market segmentation for scientific and technical information because by concentrating on these heavy users greater penetration will be achieved. He believes that this is so because the heavy half will include a strong technological gatekeeper element which will reach many who apparently do not directly make use of the library. He also sees this as a way of bridging the gap between the formal libary system and more informal methods of information transfer.

These three systems of segmentation are handicapped by an underlying disadvantage inherent in their nature. All are based on an ex-post facto analysis of the kinds of people who make up various segments of a market. They rely on *descriptive* factors rather than *causal* factors. For this reason they are not efficient predictors of future buying behaviour and it is future buying behaviour that is of central interest to marketers.

An approach to market segmentation of perhaps greater relevance to library performance assessment is the one outlined by Haley. He describes an approach, whereby it is possible to identify market segments by causal factors rather than descriptive factors which he calls benefit segmentation. The belief underlying this segmentation strategy is that the benefits which people are seeking in consuming a given product are the basic reasons for the existence of true market segments. Experience with this approach has shown that benefits sought by consumers determine their behaviour much more accurately than do demographic characteristics or volume of consumption.

Whatever basis for segmentation is selected it has also to be assumed as Hatt indicates that users are literate, have access to the library, where certain minimum environmental conditions apply and that the user has time to read.

The word user is clearly unsatisfactory in that it appears to be limited to those who use the service rather than those at whom the service is aimed. One alternative is the word customer but again this infers use of a service and another suggestion made by Wills and Oldman is to use the two words 'receiving community'. It is intended however, throughout this book to employ the word user but, assume that unless otherwise stated that it includes the potential user.

In libraries it can also frequently be asserted that there really is not such a creature as a non-user per se, as Wilson-Davis states "everyone needs and uses information to function as a member of society in any one of the multi roles a person assumes in the course of one day. What is interesting is where and how the non library users or non book buyers obtain their information". Thus although the focus of this book is on user/library interaction this will be set in the context of the other information channels to which the user is exposed.

Library usage
The term 'use' is also an imprecise one when employed in library user studies and Line (1974) attempts to clarify the situation. He defines the range of meanings encompassed by the word, emphasising the distinction between use and potential use in the same way as the user and potential user were distinguished earlier. He employs five terms to indicate the range: (i) *needs* ie what an individual ought to have; (ii) *wants* as what an individual would like to have; (iii) *demand* as what an individual asks for; (iv) *uses* as what an individual uses and (v) *requirements* as a generic term to cover all categories.

A rather more specific difficulty in defining use in the Line sense is that identified by the Bureau of Applied Social Research, where one has to be clear as to when an information seeking act begins and ends. For example does reading one book on five separate occasions count as one act or five and similarly does a single use of an index or catalogue in which five headings are searched count as one or five acts. This leads on to the difficulty of aggregating these uses if a common measure has not been employed such as time spent.

The Line distinction will largely be followed in this book. The areas of major concern here are demand and use but attempts will be made to relate these to needs and wants. The only exception to Lines definition is ironically in the term use itself, which is expanded in the context of this study to include the impact that the library use has on the user.

Libraries
King and Bryant define document transfer systems, ie libraries as "systems that transmit scientific and technical knowledge by means of document transfer systems." They go on to define documents to include published materials,

research notes, magnetic tapes, microfilms, or any other vehicle for the storage of knowledge that may be transmitted from one individual in one time frame to an individual in another. This however is a definition more of a special or university library in that it is limited to those libraries that are concerned with knowledge transmission. Nevertheless all libraries have one thing in common and that is that they are there to transmit the recorded thoughts of one individual to another individual. The narrower King and Bryant definition is perhaps more appropriate to this book, in that the field work described later does take place in two special libraries.

Let us probe a little more the concept of a special library whilst recognizing that the performance assessment question cannot be avoided in other types of library with broader goals. The methodological attraction in initially attempting to develop an assessment methodology in special libraries, is that this may point the way forward for other types of library.

At the risk of stating the obvious, special libraries are special because they serve a restricted clientele who work in an organization with comparatively specific goals. Ignoring the real problems of defining how restricted, and how specific, let us just accept this as a crude working definition which differentiates special libraries from university and public libraries. Often, too, in special libraries, a significant proportion of the documentation that it contains is of a 'hard' nature and would appear to indicate that the problems of measuring the contribution that such libraries make to corporate success are just that bit easier. Hard information in this context is defined as that information which if used, would make a direct contribution to corporate goals and which is unlikely to be used for any other purpose. The degree of unlikeliness produces the hardness indication, and use, as already indicated would not be defined, therefore, simply as distribution by the library to a given reader but defined as action as a result of assimilating information leading to a decision within the corporate framework. Simplistically, this can be seen as the difference between the university or public library manager attempting to assess the benefits that accrue from reading Tolstoy's *War and peace* and the special library manager who attempts to determine the impact that a highly technical piece of manufacturer's literature has on an engineering design decision.

TWO

THE METHODOLOGICAL PROBLEM

A BASIC and obvious methodological difficulty in establishing the value of a library is that in order to achieve this objective it entails study of the interaction of the system with the people at whom the service is aimed. Even therefore if one could meet, as Swanson points out, the scientific criteria of sameness for comparison purposes this can never be achieved absolutely even when the same people are studied in the same environment by the same methods; simply because people's perceptions and rationales change.

If however one could demonstrate that these changes in perception and rationale were negligible in their effect on the results, it is still, as Orr (1973) points out, extraordinarily difficult to develop a method that can be described in such detail that it would ensure the independent replication of results. This is because of the staggering number of variables that have to be taken into consideration in studying the effectiveness of information transfer.

Vickery (1973) for example lists over fifty variables which he groups under five major categories: environment, recipient, message, channel, and sources. More specifically in studying the message recipient one needs to consider such factors as age, education, nature of work activity, information seeking habits, stage of task, etc. In addition to these characteristics of the recipient, one needs to take into consideration the psychological make up of the recipient as Havelock et al (1969) attempts to do. They cite such factors as the degree of authoritarianism of the individual recipient, his value system, his past experiences including his fears, anxieties, insecurities and expectations. If one adds to this race, class, country of origin the list of recipient attributes becomes very daunting indeed.

Zweizig and Derwin are very dubious about the basic proposition that if we know enough about these attributes then we can predict in advance the behaviour of individuals and thus services can be planned to meet the expected needs of users:

"Say for example that there are twenty attributes that are important for predicting individual information behaviour. If these twenty attributes have only two values (eg young and old, poor and rich) the resulting combination yield 1,048,576 different types of people."

There are basically three schools of thought on the approach to human information processing and Zweizig & Derwin appear to be adherents of the unique school. The unique school, according to Driver and Mock, assume that each individual represents a unique case with respect to his mode of information processing and presumably therefore one cannot generalise at all about cognitive processes. At the other end of the spectrum is the generalist school who assume that any random sample of people can be used to make generalisations about human information processing. A third school again according to Driver and Mock is the differential school where it is recognized that people differ in cognition but that categories of people can be identified with similar thought processes on whom generalisations can be based. This is analogous to the assertion made earlier that the audience needs to be grouped into relatively homogeneous segments. The difficulty with the differential approach is how are these cognitively similar people going to be identified, and how is this information going to be applied to manage information transfer more effectively? Even if this can be resolved there is still the problem of assessing the nature of the change in that did the supplied book or information modify in some way the recipients existing knowledge? Another difficulty is to assess how the change has been achieved in terms of identifying the specific information transfer mechanism or mechanisms that were involved in the process.

Another problem is the difficulty of distinguishing

between spurious reasons for changes and real reasons which was, of course, well documented by Roethlisberger and Dickson in their Hawthorne[1] study in which they evaluated a programme designed to increase worker productivity. They found that specific programme activities, such as changes in illumination, rest periods, etc, were spuriously effective since productivity tended to increase no matter what change was made. They concluded that the true cause was the intervening variable of interest and concern on the part of management.

Suchman similarly makes the distinction between true and spurious in the field of drug testing

True Drug A ⟶ Phsysiological Changes ⟶ Reduction of disease causing condition

Spurious Act of giving Drug A ⟶ Belief in effectiveness ⟶ Relief of symptoms

Now the Suchman distinction can only be accepted if the objective of that particular evaluation was restricted to the establishment of the incidence of physiological change; many social research programmes will simply limit their research goals to the achievement of change and will therefore not be primarily concerned with how the change was achieved.[2]

Another problem set in the field of medicine but which is generally applicable is that identified by Elinson: 'If what one observes is highly variable by nature (blood pressure, a mood, the position of an electron) how can one tell whether differences in repeated measurements are due to change in the observed phenomenon or to unreliability of the method of observation'. However, if one knows, for example, that blood pressure is highly variable one must at one stage have been able to determine that variability by measurement. It is the difficulty of isolating the cause of the variability that is the problem.

---

[1] The Hawthorne conclusions have been subjected to a methodological critique by Carey who has convincingly demonstrated that the evidence collected fails to support the research findings. The Hawthorne studies are quoted here as a convenient shorthand for the favourable effect that any research investigation can have on the population being examined.

[2] Clark has produced a useful typology of different types of research where action research is defined as where it is the intention of both client and researcher to be involved in change which must be change involving the properties of the system itself.

One of the approaches to the problem of large numbers of variables is to establish a control group but there are two difficulties here, (1) the problem of establishing a control group which matches the other group in every way, (2) the administrative problems of, for example, offering a library service to one group and not the other.

Another methodological difficulty is that by investigating any situation one is likely to change that situation an obvious example of this being the 'bandwagon' effect that opinion polls appear to have on voting habits.

In information system evaluation, one needs to establish criteria by which performance can be assessed. Swanson describes criteria as performance indicators expressing specific expectation or preferences with respect to goals or events. Criteria are not measures per se, so that they do not contain units of measure but units of measure are derived from them. It is thus important to distinguish between the criterion upon which a measure is based, ie staff time saved by funding an inhouse library service and the method by which this is determined, eg simulating information seeking in a libraryless environment.

The two key methodological considerations are the questions of validity and reliability. By validity we are concerned to establish whether the criterion selected is a valid measure of, for example, a library's contribution to corporate goals. Suchman suggests a three step validity test:

1 is the criterion selected a valid criterion of what is to be measured (eg is improved job performance a valid criterion for therapeutic gains);

2 is the indicator selected a valid reflection of the gains (eg is increased production a valid criterion of improved job performance);

3 are the various valid segments of the study combined in such a way as to preserve their individual validity and achieve validity as a whole.

Reliability on the other hand is simply the degree to which results on subsequent occasions match the results of previous studies when the population and method are the same.

Another aspect of reliability is of course the issue of sampling because in user investigations it is extremely unlikely that the whole population can be studied. Thus a sample will be taken but as Brittain points out "it is not sufficient to ensure that the sampling frame includes a representative sample of users. It is also necessary to ensure that the states of research, types of data, types of information usage, channels of communication and types of user behaviour are adequately represented in the sampling frame".

According to Moser there are two objectives of any sample (1) to avoid bias and (2) achieve maximum precision for a given outlay. Bias can occur if the method of selection is non random which infers that the selection is consciously or unconsciously influenced by human choice. Thus bias in selecting the sample is avoided if the sample is chosen in a random way which requires that every member of the population has an equal chance of being picked. Bias can also occur if the sampling frame which serves as the basis for selection does not cover the population completely and if some sections of the population are impossible to locate or refuse to cooperate.

It is worth emphasising as Vickery (1973) does that "the communication system and its environment which information research must explore is vastly complex. Any single piece of research can only isolate a small element of the universe and apply a sound methodology to collect some facts about it or attempt a little theoretical clarification," The research too will be limited by the often conflicting demands of methodological purity and administrative limitation. It will also frequently be a 'one-off' investigation where clearly what is required is a series of longitudinal investigations of which the work of Tom Allen is perhaps the best example. Finally because of weaknesses of many of the techniques reviewed in the next chapter it is clearly preferable to employ several measures that converge on the same phenomenon.

THREE

SOME EVALUATIVE TECHNIQUES

Questionnaires and interviews
Libraries will, in the final analysis, be assessed on the basis of the impact that library distributed material has on the user. Inevitably this will involve therefore questioning users at some stage. This can be accomplished by interview, by telephone or indirectly through the use of mailed questionnaires.

An obvious but sometimes forgotten preliminary requirement in using these techniques is of course to be absolutely sure as to what the survey is attempting to discover and then to ensure that the questions posed are going to provide answers relevant to the surveys aims. A key stage in this process of course is the formulation of the questions to be asked. As Line (1967) has indicated one has to make questions as unambiguous as possible whilst recognising that a totally unambiguous language may result in a language that is so precise that it is utterly incomprehensible. In addition to the problem of ambiguity Peter Mann lists four other potential pitfalls: the need to avoid leading questions, double questions, jargon and emotional or threatening questions such as how much do you drink? Another problem is that many questions are aimed at determining facts about a respondents behaviour but respondents tend to have poor recall and Orr (1970) has demonstrated for example that library use can be overestimated by a factor of 20%. Clearly other methods of determining library use may be preferable but skilfull question formulation can reduce the level of misleading responses. Richardson for example suggests rephrasing the question "How many magazines do you read regularly"? to "Will you please tell me the titles of all magazines that you read regularly" even when specific titles are not required because that way you will achieve a more accurate response.

Interviews, in their most structured forms are little more than questionnaires submitted orally. However, interviews can take the conversational form, with an individual aiming to get a personal viewpoint rather than a set of responses. The spectrum ranges then from the structured or formal interview or questionnaire to the unstructured or informal interview.

The interview is clearly the most flexible means of obtaining data particularly in the nebulous world of information evaluation, but at the same time it will almost certainly be the most expensive. However one major difficulty is the distortion that can occur because of the interaction between respondent and interviewer which can be compounded if several interviewers are used.

Questionnaires on the other hand are relatively inexpensive and will frequently achieve a more representative sample. Respondents may be more frank, they have more time to produce considered answers and the problem of interviewer interaction is avoided. A key problem however with the use of questionnaires is the one of non response. King and Bryant have pointed that those who voluntarily complete a questionnaire frequently have very different characteristics from those that do not respond. Kish maintains that it is therefore important to classify non respondents in order to ascertain whether there are significant differences between respondents and non respondents. Kish also emphasizes the importance of persistence.

If the interview appears to be the preferable technique but the number of interviews have to be limited because of financial constraints, the technique of the sequential interview can be utilized. Essentially it consists of continuing to conduct interviews until only repetitive information is received. It can provide perhaps some useful qualitative information especially at the pilot stage of a project but cannot of course provide representative information. Another possibility is the use of the telephone in that it is a fairly inexpensive method of collecting data and will usually result in a high response. It, however, is inappropriate where the interview period is likely to be longer than five minutes and where some degree of probing is required, and thus is unlikely to be employed in most performance assessment studies.

Finally when the data collection method has been selected and the questions formulated the questionnaire or interview schedule will need to be carefully pilot tested ideally using a random sample of the ultimate population to be studied.

Observation
One observation technique that has been used extensively in library studies is that of work study. However as Swanson points out work study in its conventional work measurement sense is a limited technique as it only records level of effort and excludes work content, unless the nature of the work can be clearly identified by observation. It is not likely to be appropriate to the field under investigation therefore, but will tend to be restricted in its application to internal efficiency studies of the type reviewed by Masterson.

However, by utilizing a technique that has evolved from work study namely activity sampling it is possible to determine what people do rather than obtaining through questionnaires and interviews possibly misleading responses to the same question. Activity sampling is a technique in which a large number of planned instantaneous observations are made over a given period of time for a sample of the population to be studied. Each observation records what is happening at a given instant and the observations have to be sufficient in number as to be regarded as representative of the work patterns being studied. However the same problem as with work study applies, in that invariably those collecting the activity data will have to question those being observed as to the nature of the activity if this is not clear simply by observation. This can interrupt work flows and many observers may be required to preserve the statistical reliability of these observations. If one is questioning the user then the technique ceases to be observation and becomes a kind of random interview. Another disadvantage of any form of observation is the one identified by Richardson et al where one starts off as a non participant observer and ends up as a non observing participant.

Participation however can yield results as Ann Wilkin has demonstrated with her information broker studies, (the broker being distinguished from the librarian in that she is an integral part of the user group and will take part in normal assignments in addition to her information role). This is a different use of the term to that employed by Martin White and many others where an information broker is defined as one who provides information to another organization on a commercial basis.

However a variation on activity sampling which does appear to be a viable technique consists of a device which can be carried by a sample of the population which is to be studied. The device buzzes at random intervals, and the person records at that time the nature of his activity. It has the advantage too that it can be used outside normal work hours, and Disch actually eployed such a device on a recent study. The random times when the buzzer is to be sounded can be obtained from the Goodell monograph, in which tables of random times are presented.

Orr (1970) believes that this variation on activity sampling is superior to that of the diary which is reviewed in the next section because activity sampling involves little effort on the part of either the investigator or the sample population, involves minimal interference with normal work flows and is relatively free of error as there is no reliance on a participant's memory. Thus the technique would appear to be particularly helpful in building up an accurate picture of what users actually do so that information seeking habits can be related to work behaviour as a whole.

Diaries and panels
Requesting users to complete diaries is another method of establishing how users spend their time, to what information are they exposed, and what contribution the information makes to the tasks on which the users are engaged. Line (1967) however is very critical of the technique because of the difficulties of persuading a random sample of users to participate and then to ensure that those that do accept, complete the diaries for the whole study period. He maintains, because of these difficulties "the group will become even smaller and less representative if

the period over which the diaries are kept is long enough to be worthwhile, so that in the end one is left with a few individuals whose persistence is only one of their non typical features." It is worth emphasizing that even those that do stay the course will not necessarily produce diaries with reliable data. Respondents may complete the diary weekly where their recall of events that took place earlier may be hazy and in any case produce incomplete records. A variation on the diary was employed by Andrew Robertson who reports an unpublished Aslib study in which scientists and engineers were persuaded to record activities by means of a tape recorder. The amount of data produced by this approach was considerable but of course difficult to analyse. Analysis can be a problem, especially when diary records are deliberately left open ended in order to avoid prejudging the nature of the response.

Panels have been defined by H A Smith as "all techniques which make use of the same respondent on more than one occasion either on a continuous or periodic basis", and clearly the diary is one of these techniques. However according to R W Hill the "panel consists of a whole range of techniques from the continuous diary at one extreme to a follow-up postal enquiry after a single interview at the other. Continuous panels may be operated for short, medium or long periods with consumer attitudes being measured for the whole time. Periodical panels supply information for limited periods, at fixed and sometimes variable intervals of time." A key advantage thus, of the panel is the longitudinal element contrasting with the single 'snapshot' approach when only a single round of questionnaires or interviews are employed. Panels are often used where the effect of change is to be monitored, eg where the introduction of a special price offer on buying habits is to be studied.

The problems of panels are identical to of course, those encountered with the diary, ie poor initial acceptance rates from the sample, a high drop out rate, and the relatively few usable records that can be analysed at the end of the panel period. Some attempt to overcome this difficulty has been made by offering prizes or cash to panel participants that do last the course. R W Hill also mentions the technique of ensuring that the sample remains representative by topping up the sample on a quota basis, although it is not clear how this would affect the reliability of the original sample. Hill also highlights the problem of conditioning, ie that panel participants may behave differently as a result of their panel membership. This however would appear to be a problem, whatever technique is employed, and not therefore peculiar to the panel, although the panel may increase such an effect.

It will rarely be the case therefore that panels will yield representative data,[1] but they would appear still to be worth considering because of the advantages of studying the same users over a period. Also frequently the panel will yield qualitative data which can provide useful inputs to the study which can be regarded as complementary to data gathered by more representative methods.

One of the major problems of managing libraries and in conducting effective research in libraries is that they tend to be purely reactive, ie focusing most of their efforts on meeting demand. Alan Gomershall quoted in Drake clearly believes this to be the right approach to running libraries. "Successful libraries generate increasing customer business to which, by their very nature, they are obliged to respond. As a result it becomes increasingly difficult to carry out MbO or similar techniques when the individuals concerned are subjected to a widely fluctuating but increasing workload from the customer". Alan Gomershall expresses the view, perhaps only slightly tongue in cheek, that libraries could plan their services more efficiently if only they could get rid of the customers!

Basing services on demand presents two major problems:

1 clearly demand is conditioned by what is available and surely some emphasis should be placed on ascertaining needs that are not being met;

2 even if the library manager has managed to achieve a satisfactory correlation between demand patterns and corporate goals, one still has the problem of establishing a mechanism for obtaining *regular systematic* feedback into the library system so that the library remains customer responsive.

---

[1] Yorke has recently reported a panel exercise in a public library environment which appears however to have overcome some of these difficulties.

In both cases consumer panels may provide such a mechanism.

Critical incident method
The critical incident method is another approach that may yield useful qualitative data which cannot necessarily be regarded as representative. Both Davis and Ward describe the method whereby all activities relating to one project are recorded and intensively studied. In addition the incident itself can be an artificial exercise, staking place in laboratory conditions often, where one can compare the results with a 'perfect' solution.

However an authoritative paper by Flanagan on the critical incident technique defines an incident 'as any observable human activity that is sufficiently complete in itself to permit inferences and predictions to be made about the person performing the act. To be critical an incident must occur in a situation where the purpose or intent of the act seems fairly clear to the observer and where its consequences are sufficiently definite to leave little doubt abouts its effect'. Thus the technique is essentially one of *observing* behaviour in a closely defined situation and as defined by Flanagan would appear to be inapplicable to this area.

Orr (1970) rightly argues therefore that we have tended to use this term incorrectly, but I am not in favour of his suggestion that we now employ a new term namely the specific event technique. In my view the word case history is to be preferred.

Terminology aside the advantage of studying one project/event etc in depth is that it again avoids that 'snapshot' problem. It therefore enables the investigator to assess much more clearly the contribution that that information (or the absence thereof) has made to the success or failure of the project. It is again a variation on the approach of avoiding obtaining from the user group, misleading generalisations about information seeking behaviour.

Operational research
As Bookstein and Swanson indicate the "heart of the formal OR study is the creation of abstract models that represent the environment being studied". However, library

systems are very complex and the difficulties of realistic simulation stem from three factors identified by the Institute for Operational Research:

1 the complementarities and substitutabilities between different services at a micro level which interacts at the resource allocation stage and in their effect on the user;

2 the fact that systems with which we are concerned here are parts of wider information systems encompassing informal and word of mouth communication, eg, conferences and invisible colleges;

3 the variety of options open in the choice of individual components or controllable variables in information systems.

These complexities are heavily underlined by Martyn and Vickery.

It is not surprising therefore that Bookstein and Swanson state that operational research studies have tended only to be concerned with the quantity of library use that is taken as a measure of something to be optimized without regard to the quality or nature of that use. Similarly Janice Ladendorf criticises operational research for only tackling low level library goals and that operational research has made little or no contribution to evaluating total library system performance.

It is clear nevertheless that in other areas the use of models has given rise to an improvement in decision making. Adelson and Norman for example describe a typical application whereby the development of a model can optimize the location of transport depots and similar approaches can be developed for the siting of branch libraries.

It is difficult to relate this highly quantitative approach to the area covered by this book but it would be misleading to assume that operational research is not capable of simulating human behaviour. For example Schrenk reviews the impact that O.R. (operational research) has made on our understanding of decision behaviour and concludes that (1) people tend to want too much information (2) that they delay too long in arriving at decisions (3) people do not revise their decisions on the basis of new information and thus tend to give too much weight to early information (4) that despite this limitation in human decision performance people generally compare favourably with optimum solutions.

However, Martyn and Vickery maintain that "attempts to design a predictive model which will enable an optimally performing information system to be constructed in a single operation for a given user population are impracticable". They conclude that the contribution of O.R. would therefore be limited to an array of specialised models each useful in predicting a small subset of these variables; a notional system might then be designed using each model to suggest a configuration which would be optimal as assessed by each variable or subset of variables in turn.

It would be hoped therefore that more empirical work on the impact of the outputs of a library system would enable one to develop a specialized model of the kind described by Martyn and Vickery, although it would be wrong to underestimate the difficulties of establishing a viable predictive model because of the problems outlined earlier.

FOUR

APPROACHES TO LIBRARY PERFORMANCE ASSESSMENT

Cost Benefit Analysis and Pricing
The value of a system as has been previously stated is according to Vickery (1973) the 'degree to which the system contributes to user needs. If the value can be expressed in monetary terms and compared with cost, this then becomes a cost benefit anlaysis." Cost benefit evaluation is thus according to Lancaster (1977) concerned with whether the value of a service is more or less than the cost of providing it. In other words a cost benefit study attempts to determine whether the expense of providing a service is justified by the benefits derived from it. Wolfe et al assert that "cost benefit analysis is concerned with maximising the social[1] output per unit of input, that is, imposing the same efficiency criteria on the public or non market sector that a perfectly competitive price system is said to impose on the private sector". Flowerdew and Whitehead have stated that "the definition and evaluation of the costs of providing information is one half, the simpler half of the problem of obtaining a cost benefit measure[2] and has previously stated will largely be ignored in this book.

---

[1] One difficulty here is to distinguish between social and personal benefits in that individuals may appear to value services highly that are not perhaps significantly contributing to societal or corporate goals whilst others that are not valued as highly are.

[2] Notwithstanding this I would query one statement they make on sunk costs, ie, where a lease forbids subletting according to Flowerdew & Whitehead the cost of library space should be regarded as nil. However I would argue that the library by occupying this space is putting pressure on the host organisation and thus the library should be charged the full economic rent.

Cost benefit analysis therefore attempts to set out and evaluate social costs, and social benefits of an investment. As Wolfe states "a distinguishing factor between profit maximisation in the private sector and welfare maximisation in the public sector is the inclusion of externalities in the decision making criterion of the latter. Profit maximising firms will consider only the returns and costs borne by them whereas welfare maximising public decisions must include in the decision calculus the external or spillover benefits and costs that accrue to other parties." Thus in calculating the benefits of constructing an underground railway as well as taking into account the revenue from ticket sales the analysis would also include reduced travelling times for users and reductions in traffic congestion. Frost perceives cost benefit analysis as a choice between two alternatives, in library management terms; this could be seen as a choice between investing in a library or utilizing the money in some other way. However, more likely the choice should really be seen more in terms of which library services are making a corporate contribution and which are not. Frost also makes the important point that in evaluating two alternatives each solution is sub-optimized in that it represents the most efficient arrangement possible for both alternatives. Layard (and many other commentators) emphasize two other important considerations in conducting a cost benefit analysis:

1 the relative valuation of costs and benefits occurring at different points in time, the problem of time preference, and the opportunity cost of capital; and

2 the valuation of costs and benefits accruing to people with different incomes.

One suggested method of establishing the benefit is to ascertain what people are prepared to pay for a service. This approach has a number of weaknesses:

(i) as Flowerdew and Whitehead point out "willingness to purchase an information service at a particular price only reveals that the purchaser values the information at that price or more. The price may therefore not measure the full benefit to the purchaser".

(ii) there is the general problem of the attitude of society towards information as Wolfe again indicates "what are the forces that have caused the provision of total secondary information services to come largely into non-private hands. Partly these forces are historical; the information field has to some extent developed out of the public library service. The existence of free information provision in some areas and the constant growth of the scope of such provision must necessarily cause any private entrepreneur to hesitate before launching an information agency." Thus it is difficult to establish benefits of any public sector/non market services because one has no comparison to draw upon as to what people are prepared to pay for a similar service in the private sector. Newton emphasises these dangers in a recreational study where the benefit of a public beach was judged on the basis of what people are prepared to pay for an equivalent private beach. "The main difficulty here is that private recreation facilities tend to offer a different service namely exclusiveness and another problem arises by virtue of the fact that public facilities are provided free of charge and this tends to force downwards the price of private facilities". What is more there must be an historical factor that applies here particularly to libraries, ie this has always been free so why should I pay for it? This historical attitudinal factor may well depress any shadow prices (or real come to that), that the cost benefit analyst may care to determine from potential users *even when the service is highly valued;*

(iii) what people are prepared to pay for is not the same as what people *say* they are prepared to pay. Wolfe yet again "economists have in the past been reluctant to rely upon surveys of consumer expressed preferences. They have mainly inclined to the view that only choice revealed in the market could offer evidence about consumers' underlying preferences". Similarly, decision theorists such as Marschak and Radner maintain that definitions of decision preferences should be based on observing action (he has chosen A when B was available), rather than on recording verbal statements (he has said I prefer A to B);

(iv) special libraries are not generally companies engaged in the selling of information in the open market so inevitably any attempt to introduce a form of shadow pricing is as difficult as the whole problem of allocating overheads. A British Institute of Management research report by Melrose-Woodman indicates that most overheads which would almost certainly include library expenditure are simply apportioned on some arbitrary basis, ie, invoice sales or capital employed of the division to whom the service is offered and not on actual use of the overhead service. Where overhead costs are allocated on an actual use basis, the difficulty in library terms is to maintain records that allow for the costs to be allocated in this way. Library budgets in the context of overall overhead costs would not in practice provide a discriminatory pricing mechanism, because the individual library user will frequently be unaware of the transfer payment that is being made on his behalf to the library for the service given. Even if he is aware of the allocation system, he is still unlikely to make the conscious decision as to whether use of the service is worth the price that he is being charged, especially as the money is internal and not treated in as critical a fashion as 'real' money used to purchase services outside the firm;

(v) Marcus too, considers that real money is no more objective than any other scale of value. Layard also emphasises this when he states that "the only basic principle is that we should be willing to assign numerical values to costs and benefits and arrive at decisions by adding them up and accepting those projects whose benefits exceed their costs". However although this is a theoretically defensible position it really does not help. If one is talking about library costs they will inevitably be expressed in monetary terms and therefore to make the comparison meaningful the benefits should also be expressed in monetary terms.

Some of the ways of assigning money values to the use of library services are somewhat critically reviewed in this book and it is my view that our first priority is that we should establish a methodology for assessing the value (in Vickery's sense) of how well the library system is meeting user needs/ corporate goals. Once value has been established, then we can produce cost *per* benefit data, perhaps as an intermediary step to the production of true cost benefit data, where money values are actually assigned to library benefit data;

(vi) Zais points out that there is another problem in applying market economics to libraries in that there is an inherent conflict in pricing policies which on one hand attempt to recover costs whilst on the other charge prices that yield the most social benefit;

(vii) it has also been suggested by Zais that the technique of marginal cost pricing may be applicable to information in that its basic objective is to maximise net social benefits. For libraries operating in the public sector particularly, this would appear to be a possibility. However, However, the marginal cost price is set on the assumption that all output is sold. How this concept would be applied to libraries whose output is reuseable is something that I frankly don't understand.

It has been pointed out however by Ford (1977) that "while public and academic libraries usually make no charges for their services, they do have pricing policies. These are largely expressed in terms of loan policies and internal arrangements. Thus a short loan period — say four hours — can be regarded as a high price and a long loan period as a low price." Thus pricing can be seen simply as a rationing technique, and an attempt to directly involve users in the establishment of such a shadow pricing policy was made by Blagden (1973).

It is suggested therefore that whatever pricing system is used, unless it is employed in the open market place; will not shed much light on how well the service is meeting user needs. Pricing can however be helpful in those rare situations where an equivalent service is available in the open market place from which a value for the in house service can be derived. Internal non market pricing systems either trying to simulate the open market or providing a mechanism for the transfer of the costs of an inhouse library would not appear to be an adequate measure therefore, of a special library's corporate contribution.

McDonough emphasizes the explicit rationale for investing in an information system. "Either much better decisions should result or the decision requirements on the individual should have been reduced. The system should now be carrying some of the workload previously carried by the individual. In the case of better decisions the costs of the system are justified in this improvement. In the case of reduced requirement on the individual the job has been de-skilled and this is susceptible to lower salary positioning."

Clearly this is a yardstick by which the system can be judged but statements of this sort derived from information economics do not provide a method by which the improvements in decision making outlined by McDonough can be established. Thus cost benefit analysis provides some assistance to those engaged in library performance assessment eg when comparing alternatives both should be sub optimized and that the analysis should take into account all costs and all benefits. Pricing too can be useful where similar services are offered on a commercial basis, outside the library's host organization.

Generally however libraries do not operate in the market place and this is where in the author's view both user charging and overhead transfer payments fall down. Cost benefit analysis has not therefore got us to the stage where we can put a money figure on the value of library services and neither does it suggest how this can be achieved.

Time saved justificatory data
It has been argued that money values can be assigned to the use of libraries on the basis of the time that a library service saves the user of that service. King and Bryant are quite categoric about this when they state that if there is any economic advantage in using a human intermediary in the document screening process, the source of the advantage must lie in either a saving of manpower costs, service costs or both. Such a statement however does exclude any advantages that are gained from a library in terms of the quality of answer or material that it distributes to a user.

King and Bryant also maintain that these savings in manpower costs can be effected through a differential in the pay scales of the user and the screener or in the speed with which screening decisions can be made. Saving in service costs can be accommodated if the amount of photocopying, postage and other communication costs can be reduced by supplying the user with only a subset of the system's output.

Clearly there are potential time penalties as Flowerdew and Whitehead indicate if information is not provided or is inadequate:

1 do without and work perhaps less productively for the same number of research hours;

2 spend research time in obtaining information for himself with consequent reductions in output;

3 work longer hours to collect information for himself.
However there are four major difficulties in quantifying the benefits of time savings:
(i) Frost maintains that it can be extremely misleading to use values of time obtained in one context for the evaluation of savings in another. For example, presumably a person would be prepared to pay more to avoid an extra five minutes in a dentist's chair having a tooth drilled by a slow machine than he would to avoid an extra five minute delay in being serviced in a restaurant;
(ii) it is probably false to assume that time savings can be linearly aggregated, eg twelve five-minute savings equal one hour saved, as there is evidence to suggest that short time savings are relatively worthless;
(iii) Harrison and Quarmby also mention the problem that "for some classes of worker no distinction can be drawn between working and non working time, ie those who are paid according to work done may simply prefer more leisure time or some combination of the two";
(iv) even if the saved time can be translated into higher productivity levels they will not always result in reduced manpower costs because of the difficulties associated with redundancies and redeployment.
Notwithstanding these major objections, time saved is still one of the standard special library justifications despite the fact that such justifications are unable to answer the question raised by Judge: "at what point the cost of obtaining information for a better decision becomes uneconomic in relation to the benefits obtained".

Thus time saved calculations do not give any indication of the value of the information supplied, ie, it is assumed that the information is entirely relevant to corporate objectives. In addition it is frequently assumed that all time saved is used productively. Finally methods of ascertaining these time savings would appear to be unreliable and some of the attempts that have been made are reviewed in the next chapter.

User satisfaction and the use of libraries
Although this may appear slightly fanciful it is difficult to discover any evidence which demonstrates that a satisfactory correlation exists between generalised assessments

of user satisfaction and the performance of a library; this is apart from the major difficulties of actually measuring satisfaction and the problems of including non or infrequent users. According to Wills and Oldman two key problems associated with attitude measurement are (1) "the nature of the relationship between attitude and behaviour and (2) the direction of any relationship between attitude and behaviour. Does a favourable attitude lead to use of a library service or alternatively an unfavourable one to non use and does an attitude change necessarily precede behaviour or vice versa. Burr and Wessel (1968) however both argue for the application of utility analysis to library management problems, although Wessel admits that "utility analysis depends upon the concept that the consumer not only knows that he prefers A to B but he can give numerical expression to his desires which permits him to say he prefers A, say, twice as much as B, giving A twice the utility of B". However this approach has been discarded by welfare economists from whom it was drawn because of the difficulties of measuring even one person's satisfaction and the consequent aggregation difficulties that such data would inevitably produce.

It can of course be argued that use of a library is in itself an indicator of satisfaction and King and Bryant agree with this by assuming that users can verbally characterise their needs for information found in documents. Burnett, however, takes an altogether different view: "the consumer does not always know or ask for what he needs and what he wants may not always be in his own best interests so that one cannot accept the sovereignty of readers without reservation". This point is underlined by Stecher who states "obviously effectiveness is not reflected merely by a measure of the successful use of the library. It may well be that a valid indicator of effectiveness will involve a ratio of successful to unsuccessful use or even a ratio of manifest to latent demand". A different view is expressed however by Totterdell & Bird who agree that counts of issues or users are not in themselves measure of effectiveness, but it is surely reasonable to assume that a user will visit the library and borrow an item because he feels it is likely to meet a particular need that he is aware that he has. Admittedly the user may subsequently find the book has failed to provide him with what he wanted. However, if this occurred regularly the user would be expected eventually to cease to make attempts to meet his need at libraries.

However if the Totterdell & Bird assumption is accepted data would still have to be collected on frequency of use, time in membership, lapsed members to indicate more specifically how effective usage is. In addition of course if the maximising of use is the overriding goal of libraries then from where are the extra resources going to be obtained to support those libraries that successfully pursue these policies. Surely success will inevitably lead to failure as demand exceeds capacity of available resources. This frequently moves one towards the situation identified by Drucker, to which reference was made earlier, where performance is judged simply on the basis of the ability of a library manager to maintain or increase his budget. A theme of this book is that one should attempt to bring these two strands of librarianship much closer together so that budget allocations and beneficial usage strategies are in closer harmony with each other.

Advertising, like librarianship, faces a similar difficulty in relating attitude to behaviour, as Voos points out: "unfortunately we do not know whether prospective buyers actually use the information obtained by reading an advertisement to make decisions nor do we know whether they did any actual purchasing". However the ultimate aim of advertising is to stimulate the sales of the product that is being advertised and that is something which can be measured, as can the number of people exposed to a particular advertisement. We have therefore a similar problem in establishing a connection between library activities and what we are ultimately trying to achieve.

Generalised attitude surveys can of course have useful propaganda value as witness the Library Association's extensive quotations from the Daily Mail survey in their fight against the cuts. Those engaged in library attitude studies would presumably argue that plotting levels of satisfaction will give an indication of the degree of cognitive enrichment achieved by the library user. In addition favourable attitudes will influence budget allocation and strengthen the library's status in the organisation. Attitudes are an important ingredient in the disposition to use information but the measurement of these attitudes should be capable of validation against specific information seeking acts. Generalised data as in other sections of this study, would often appear to be misleading, as Moriarty using a Remmers Kelly scale found that there appeared to be little difference in user attitudes towards well stocked, well staffed university libraries, and modestly stocked, modestly staffed high school libraries. Similarly Barr in the field of education evaluation also reports little correlation between teacher rating of pupils and actual learning improvements.

More recently Totterdell and Bird have shown that there would not appear to be marked differences in the attitudes of non reader and readers, and public library users and non users, towards a number of library related statements generated by the Likert technique [1] If it is reasonable to infer from the Totterdell and Bird study that people do not in general have strong attitudes towards libraries then a very sensitive measuring device will be required to indicate subtle attitudinal differences. If these tools do exist then they will also require considerable expertise in their application.

Another dimension of user satisfaction is the homeostatic effect which has been observed by Buckland, and many others working at Lancaster University. Satisfaction levels here were plotted against the availability of material thus if one improves the availability of material one also, after a short period, increases the satisfaction of the user. Satisfaction levels initially go up but after a period, the higher expectations reduce the satisfaction levels. Similarly I can recall Edward Dudley recounting an incident at Hampstead Public Library where strenuous efforts were made to upgrade the stock in certain subjects. Again this attracted criticism from some users because the improved collection had stimulated their interest, but had failed to meet their increased expectation.

Attitudes are commonly measured by scale where as Triandis points out it is assumed that an attitude can be arranged along a single dimension from very pro to very

---

[1] Lubans too (quoted in Ford 1977) has also shown that non users differ little or at all in respect of all other characteristics with library users.

con; whilst respondents attitudes are unlikely to be that straightforward. In addition if one is restricted to the measurement of attitude (usually on a one off basis) no insight will be provided as to the factors that led to the development of this attitude. Another problem with attitude studies (even those concerned with assessing attitudes towards specific services or output) is the one identified by Roy Knight who cites three examples as to why a customer could record dissatisfaction with a library information service:

1 a correct negative to an unanswerable question;

2 not being able to answer at the time but could have done if time allowed;

3 not a satisfactory answer to the user even though the answer was correct;

none of which necessarily indicate an inadequate library service.

As Line (1967) asserts "the fact that 60% of users thought the library poor means neither more nor less than that a majority thought the library poor, it does not mean (it may suggest) that the library is poor". Christine Oldman (1976) points out that in any case good and bad are hardly objective concepts and emphasizes greater interest in user perception of good and bad. Whilst freely admitting the massive subjectivity of this area it is still difficult to relate attitudinal data to 'objective' performance evaluation measures and thus such data is difficult to operationalise as Oldman frankly admits. If one is concerned with the performance of the library system as a whole there is also the difficulty of relating attitudes to a wide range of library services.

In short therefore attitudes towards library services and purely quantitative indications of the use of a library can serve as helpful ammunition in defending a library's position. They generally however do not give much help to the library manager in guiding her as to what changes should be made to the system to improve performance.

Relevance

'The operation in such documentation centres have for a long time been seen from a pragmatic view stressing the question of relevance. All experimental work at Cranfield is directed primarily to investigating the relevance concept. The results of the information must be relevant, it has been said.

However, anyone who stresses relevance as a criterion must answer the question- relevant to whom and for what purpose? We seem here to be trapped in the same situation as many economists who discuss utility or value in economics. The economist has developed important tools and methods without settling this question.' Eleven years on after Tell made this comment it would appear that the questions relevant to whom and for what purpose are unanswered despite the plethora of relevance studies.

Elwen points out that the original concept of relevance is that of 'logical relevance or topic appropriateness which has to do with whether or not a document contains information on a subject which has some topical bearing on the information need expressed in the question'. Hannah also indicated that "relevance was viewed as the result of a match between the terms of question and the terms of an index. This led to consideration of the relevance. Relevance was considered to be the property of the internal organisation of the system and of the documents included in the system. It appeared as if one could arrange a matching between questions and relevant answers solely by system manipulation."

Elwen describes how the concept of pertinency emerged, contrasting relevance as being associated with the relationship between a document and a question "whereas pertinency is associated with the information need of which the question is a formal representation. It must also be realised that a gap exists between what the user says he wants and what he actually wants so that the degree to which relevancy and pertinency overlap depends upon the ability of the user to express his needs effectively."

Similarly Rees and Schulze in a comprehensive series of relevance investigations make the distinction between relevance and usefulness, which Cooper calls the relevance theoretic measure and the utility theoretic measure of a system's effectiveness. Cooper also maintains that the advantage of the utility approach is that there is only one fundamental measure of utility, namely the number of utiles received by the user population as a result of using the system. It is not clear however how these utiles would be defined and aggregated for a given user population. Even assuming that these problems are satisfactorily resolved it does also assume that a favourable judgement of a document's pertinency indicates that this can be equated with corporate contribution. Cooper suggests in a letter that if the objective of a retrieval system is to please someone other than the immediate user the user himself is still the best person to make that judgement. However Driver and Mock point out that psychological and human information processing research has shown that users invariably prefer more data even past the point of the maximum level of information processing and conceptual abstraction. Thus users capacity for and preference for information do not seem to coincide.

One possible explanation for the lack of progress on measuring the relevance of a system's output to corporate goals (in addition to methodological problems) is that many relevance studies have taken place in academic and research organisations where it presumably is assumed that individual and corporate goals are in harmony. Saracevic, in a wide ranging review of the relevance concept, has identified seven different approaches to the problem of measuring relevance and emphasizes that these different approaches are not mutually exclusive. However although Saracevic provides the framework, relevance investigations have not as yet established a methodology for assessing the relevance of a system's output to corporate goals.

FIVE

A REVIEW OF SOME MAJOR STUDIES

A REVIEW of some of the significant work in the field is now presented in which the techniques and evaluative approaches described earlier have been employed.

The Allen investigations

Allen studied the use of communication channels in research and development teams and their relationship with problem solution and ultimately overall technical performance. He studied communication patterns in a number of twinned projects, ie, where a government agency deliberately allocates the same research remit to two different organisations. He was therefore able to compare performance in two organisations working on the same task. Allen was also able to employ a super judge, in this case the government agency funding the contract, to provide a more objective evaluation of performance.

The studies were conducted on the basis of recording messages received by those working on the team, the source of these messages and the contribution that these messages made to the solution of the problem. He collected his data by four methods:

1 a time allocation form which was essentially a simple diary record completed each week by all project engineers on which all activities were recorded;

2 regular interviews with members of the project team;

3 periodic tape recorded progress reports;

4 the solution development record[1] which plotted

---

[1]McAlpine believes that the s.d.r. can only be used where the problem can be precisely defined.

alternative solution probabilities until one alternative was selected and the other discarded. Collecting these probabilities over a period of time provided a graphic method of a project's history. On the back of the form sources of significant messages were recorded.

The key conclusions of these studies were:

1 that no relation exists between channel value and channel selection and this undoubtedly is yet another confirmation of the Zipf principle[1] of least effort, which has frequently been reported (Victor Rosenberg, Stecher & R S Taylor) that ease of access is more important than the quality of information obtained. However Allen (1977) reports that accessibility is influenced by the degree of experience an engineer has with a given channel. Of course the engineer may simply refer more frequently to those channels that he considers easier to use. In other words the direction of causality may be from accessibility to experience. Allen determined causal direction by controlling the use by engineers of channels and correlating experience and perceived accessibility. Although correlation is not quite so strong Allen is confident that the degree of experience that an engineer acquires with an information channel does tend to lower his perception of the cost of using that channel;

2 the performance of literature is at best mediocre on the basis of the analysis of the source of messages which in turn were correlated with performance. No information was given in the Allen studies as to the nature of the library services which supported these projects. The unanswered questions here are therefore: was the mediocre performance of the literature due to the wrong literature being supplied to the project engineers because of some failure in the library service, in terms of accessibility, staffing, funding level etc, *or*, was mediocre performance due to the fact that in the particular environment studied, literature was inappropriate to prototype design work?

It is interesting to note here that in Table 2 reproduced earlier there is this surprising similarity in the amount of time engineers spend on literature. This may suggest that there is some general characteristic applying here either for example

---

[1] Psychological costs affect this principle as well in that users will go outside for information to avoid revealing ignorance to colleagues.

in terms of the nature of the work or the characteristics of engineers which produce these consistent work patterns;
3 higher performers rely more on internal sources;
4 informal communication via the technological gatekeeper can overcome the organisational impediments to the flow of information. These technological gatekeepers were identified by plotting communication networks[1] and these communication stars appeared according to Allen (1970) to have the following characteristics (1) more outward looking (2) they read more (3) they maintain long term relationships with technologists outside the organisation and in short they provide a crucial technological link between the outside world and their organisational colleagues.

The Allen investigation has a number of advantages over many other studies in that it: (1) was of a longitudinal nature conducted in a number of environments and (6) employed a range of different methods and thus to some extent was able to combine the advantages of the sample survey and the intensive single case method. Data was gathered during the life of a project reducing the errors due to faulty recall (according to Line (1967) recollection tends to fall away sharply after three months).

A possible reservation about the Allen work is the emphasis on significant messages. In the solution development record it specifically requests respondents to record "information which has a *serious* (my emphasis) impact upon your visualization of the problem or any of its potential solutions". The problem with this approach is that it ignores the supportive but relatively insignificant sources that led up to this important message, thus possibly underestimating the value of some sources.

This was certainly recognised by Allen (1977) when he asserted that significant ideas rarely came fully blown from one source and invariably several sources suggested parts of the idea. Where this was the case however, Allen gave credit to all sources.

The mediocre performance of literature can be reduced somewhat by the fact that the technological gatekeepers

---

[1] A study by Ritchie and Hindle building on the work of Allen has now established an effective way of networking communication patterns within an organization.

read more than their colleagues, and presumably communicated the results of this reading to their colleagues. Another difficulty with the Allen data is that performance quite rightly is based on what the team produces at the end of the project. When the team's usage of literature as a whole is correlated with performance, it may give a mediocre correlation which disguises some high reading and high individual performances. Allen was certainly also aware of this and did correlate a number of subsystem solutions with channel usage and still found no correlation between use of literature and quality of solution. I have not been able to ascertain, however, whether subsystem solutions were only worked on by one individual, because, if not, the same reservations would apply. In addition by emphasizing solutions Allen perhaps tends to detract from the benefits that literature confers in terms of thought clarification and problem definition.

Allen has demonstrated how engineers or certainly space/aeronautic and electronic engineers differ from their scientific colleagues in their communication patterns. His studies have emphasised the importance of accessibility both in terms of ease of use and other perceived psychological barriers to channel usage. He has convincingly demonstrated the existence of the technological gatekeeper and has stressed the importance of stimulating the use of internal consultants. Above all he has set high methodological standards which should be of considerable utility to future studies of information transfer.

The Cranfield studies
The fieldwork which formed the basis of these studies was conducted at two universities, the Cranfield Institute of Technology and Loughborough University of Technology. It was a methodological investigation attempting to make a contribution to the problems involved in evaluating the performance of libraries.

As has been indicated earlier Oldman (1976) had rejected any quasi measures of good and bad and was only concerned with users' perception of good and bad. These subjective assessments were gathered by first establishing data on respondents initial expectation of the two libraries before they had used the libraries, and how this expectation altered over a period of time when the libraries were used.

This approach is based on the work of Martin Fishbein who constructed the following formula

$$DV = \frac{Per\ Act}{Exp}$$

where Exp = expectations, where Per Act = perceived actualisation, where DV = derived value.

It has also much in common with the work conducted at Lancaster University and documented in the Buckland publication. However no attempt was made at Cranfield to record changes in satisfaction levels resulting in different levels of provision.

The Cranfield attitudinal data was collected by questionnaire in which respondents were asked to register their degree of agreement/disagreement with a number of statements, (a technique originally developed by Likert), plus a number of other questions on other aspects of user attitudes and potential behaviour.

In the Oldman (1978) thesis therefore where these studies are reported a large amount of attitudinal data is presented, showing how the initial user expectation of library services alters over a period of time. An example from the thesis is illustrated overleaf.

The problems with this data are:

1 the numbers in each category are very small and certainly therefore unrepresentative;

2 even if they were representative would sharply defined attitudinal differences have emerged?;

3 most fundamental of all, there is clearly no guarantee whatsoever that these statements are necessarily reflected in behaviour. Did the people strongly agreeing in Table 3 actually use or not use the library because it was too noisy or too quiet? Certainly if I wanted to investigate that particular issue, the Fishbein approach would not be the one that I would select.

This data was supplemented by establishing a panel of respondents from whom data was collected over a period of time. The object of the panel was according to Wills and Oldman "to understand the derivation of value from library

Table 3 A library should be a place where one can concentrate and get some work done.

Time Period	Strongly agree Mgrs. %	Strongly agree Mech. Eng. %	Slightly agree Mgrs. %	Slightly agree Mech. Eng. %	Neither agree nor disagree Mgrs. %	Neither agree nor disagree Mech.Eng. %	Slightly disagree Mgrs. %	Slightly disagree Mech.Eng. %	Strongly disagree Mgrs. %	Strongly disagree Mech.Eng. %
Initial user expectation	39.1	54.3	31.3	21.7	18.2	15.2	7.8	8.6	3.5	0.0
2	7.6	17.3	24.6	36.9	27.1	13.0	23.7	19.5	16.9	8.6
3	7.8	26.3	25.7	37.4	20.0	18.4	26.9	13.1	20.0	7.8
4	8.8	11.6	27.4	32.5	24.5	23.9	23.5	11.6	25.5	16.2
5	12.9	17.2	27.9	31.0	19.3	20.6	26.8	13.7	16.1	13.7

services by studying the individuals' total information behaviour over time".

The panel utilized in this investigation consisted of a diary in which respondents were asked to log their educational tasks and the information sought and acquired for the solution of these tasks. The researchers were of course aware of two of the major problems associated with the diary, namely conditioning and mortality. It is very difficult, if not impossible, to establish whether the diarists behave differently because of their participation in the project. However although twelve panel members' library use was recorded, no analysis appears to have been conducted to compare their usage pattern with a control group of non diarists, in an attempt to establish whether use was affected by diary completion. Panel dropouts were the other major problem in the thirteen week Cranfield diary exercise. A random group of management students were invited to join the panel and there was a 75% acceptance, almost half of which had dropped out by the beginning of the second term (about halfway through the study). At Loughborough this was overcome by reducing the period of study from thirteen weeks to six weeks, where the drop out rate was insignificant (although the acceptance rate is not given).

The Cranfield studies did produce a benefit typology that users might expect from a library and these are reproduced below.

1 *The reactive library* able to react effectively on known-item searches.

2 *The pro-active library* able to interact professionally with the user in his own interest area.

3 *The equi-marginal library* able to play an equal part in planning jointly with leaders of other information media, eg, the teacher, to seek an equi-marginal contribution from informative artefacts to the overall knowledge or learning goals of an organisation.

4 *The serendipitous library* able to afford browsing capability in a planned manner to facilitate a pro-active relationship with the information artefacts (as distinct from (2) where the pro-activity is between professional staff and user).

5 *The archival library* able to serve as a permanent

source of record of storehouse for 'all' information artefacts on the assumption that they might well be needed at some time in the future, typically with the user searching on his own behalf.

This classification of benefits was based however on the researchers own perceptions rather than, as far as I could ascertain, the attitudinal data collected in the field. This is a pity, because it would have been interesting to discover academic staff attitudes to involving the librarian in, for example, course planning. Notwithstanding that, there would also appear to be more effective methods of obtaining user input to a library benefit achievement strategy, for example by observing browser behaviour and by questioning users, rather than recording attitudes towards the concept of a serendipitous library.

It was interesting to learn that heavy users of the library were either academic high fliers or students who were so unsure of themselves that they felt the need to acquire information additional to that recommended.

My interest in this statement is twofold:

1 it demonstrates that not all library use is beneficial and, in the case of the unsure student, whether it is possible for a perceptive librarian to liaise with the academic staff to give an early warning of this student's difficulty;

2 it also demonstrates that top academic performers do use literature heavily, perhaps slightly contrasting with Tables 1 and 2 where there appeared to be a uniformity of information use by both high and low performers.

It was disappointing therefore to discover that this research finding was not supported by any data, as it would have been interesting to have seen how these high users fitted into the overall library usage patterns. It would also have been interesting to learn how usage patterns, student ratings, and library failures were methodologically determined. Finally it would have been worthwhile to conduct an analysis of these failures to ascertain what changes in the management of these two libraries should be made.

This last point really underlines my reservations about this work in that it is difficult to see how attitudinal data can be utilized by the practising library manager. The Cranfield studies therefore have largely reinforced by bias (prejudice?) against studies of this sort, to which reference was made in Chapter 4.

Certainly however the detailed information available on the use of a diary for collecting library usage data is worth examining as it indicates in practical terms some of the difficulties and advantages of using this method.

Document delivery

An attempt to develop a more objective tool has resulted in the concept of document delivery. According to Lancaster (1977) there are two major approaches to evaluating libraries in terms of their ability to deliver documents:

1 the use of some type of citation pool from which a sample of citations is drawn and used to test the document delivery capabilities of a number of libraries;

2 the use of some type of survey, wherein actual needs of a sample of library users are identified, and the library is tested on its ability to satisfy these needs.

In both cases a library's delivery capability is compared with that of a perfect library which has everything demanded, immediately available.

A difficulty in applying this quasi-objective measure is as Orr frankly admits "users learn the strengths and weaknesses of a library's collection and if there are alternative sources for the documents it does not own, they often turn to these sources without making their needs known to the library staff. A library that is able to fill all but a small percentage of the needs its users make known, therefore, can either be a library that actually does have everything its users need or one that is by-passed except for the particular needs it can fill".

This is why Orr and his co-workers favoured the first approach identified by Lancaster of basing delivery evaluation on 'objective' lists compiled by experts or by counts of citation frequency. However as Oldman (1976) points out it can be a self-reinforcing situation in that the most cited journals are the most available journals and are therefore most likely to be cited again.

Orr attempts to define user needs, ie, the document universe of the user population, by the indirect method of examining the citations of those research workers that publish papers; the assumption being that the ones they cite are the ones they have read. Again, Orr freely admits that this poses a number of problems, in that it: (1) tends to exclude review papers as authors will be inclined to cite only primary works (2) will include relevant references and not irrelevant papers (3) excludes non-author users (4) is biased towards older material. However, Orr also argues that as research needs are more difficult to meet it is likely to underestimate the capability rather than overestimate it.

In order to combat any conditioning effect of library stock on citation patterns Orr also took a sample of research workers and their publications from a medical research directory. When the lists are compiled, the time taken to deliver is either actually measured or, what appears to be more frequently the case, it is assumed that if an item is, for example, not in stock this is likely to take x amount of time to deliver. Clearly, actual times are preferable to assumed times, but apparently the standard times are based on a number of replicated studies of actual times.

Buckland (1974) is critical of the Orr approach for the additional reason that he is highly sceptical of the proposition that searching by professional librarians from another library is equivalent to the search behaviour of researchers who are not professional librarians. Another limitation of document delivery identified by Lancaster is that while it is simple to apply, the scoring system becomes quite complicated when the test is attempted in a large library system, eg a university library comprising a main library and multiple departmental libraries.

Although the citations are all selected from medical sources, this would not, one would assume, necessarily produce only references to medical literature. However, assuming that the subject field of medicine can be limited in some way, it would have seemed reasonable to exclude items that fall outside the area, or at least the area that the library claimed to be covering. In other words, is it reasonable to penalise the library in terms of document delivery capability for not stocking a particular title which was *deliberately* excluded as an acquisition. It is well known for example that there is a Pareto type relationship between a library's stock and its customers, in that frequently 80% of the requests will be satisfied by 20% of the stock. Most

UK special libraries recognise that they cannot be remotely self-sufficient and thus will be explicitly or implicitly managed to exploit the Pareto phenomenon.

An example of the alternative approach to document delivery was identified by Line (1973) where he wished to establish why users do not come to the library to seek bibliographical material. Participants in the Line study were asked to record references of interest over a period and the library's success in obtaining these references was measured in a similar way to that employed by Orr.

Both these approaches are based on a library's ability to deliver known documents and does not test its ability to provide titles or information in response to subject requests. Also this approach again, assumes that only that title will do when there may be a title sitting on the shelf immediately available, which would have served the user equally well.

Orr has developed a sound technique for measuring a library's capability to deliver documents, although delivery in itself does not guarantee corporate contribution. However a library will not contribute to corporate goals unless a document or information from a document is delivered to a user. Thus document delivery is a useful intermediate technique for evaluating one aspect of library performance.

Failure analysis
A variation on the theme of analysing the success of readers (as opposed to total populations served) in obtaining known titles was conducted by Urquhart and Schofield who analysed reader failures. The failures were analysed by user and by subject and the subject analysis was correlated with the subject strength of the stock. This was a study of actual failure, rather than the artificially produced lists that Orr used, but it again over emphasizes, from the special library viewpoint, the known title approach, ie, it assumes that only that title will do. Also it again assumes that all books sought ought to be supplied.

Collection evaluation in general
Both the work of Orr, and Urquhart and Schofield, concentrate on two specific aspects of the ability of the

stock of a library to meet certain user requirements. Bonn however in a comprehensive review of collection evaluation methods lists a number of other criteria for evaluating the stock of a library: (1) straight size counts (2) budget size or budget expressed as a ratio of total university budget or expenditure per head of user etc (3) subject balance (4) unfulfilled requests (5) inter library loans (6) standard lists (7) user opinion of stock and, of course, (8) document delivery capabilities.

A more systematic attempt to evaluate the adequacy of a university library's stock was that proposed by Clapp and Jordan. They confirm that the adequacy of an academic collection can be simply measured by the size of the collection but size will depend on size and composition of the faculty and student body, curriculum, methods of instruction, geographic location of the campus and other physical facilities. They therefore have developed a formula by which these factors can be included and thus the adequacy of the collection more effectively evaluated.

The problem with the approach of Clapp and Jordan and many of the other criteria identified by Bonn is that as Hamburg et al assert, it is based mainly on input to the library system rather than output or benefit to the user.

Benefit inversion
Hawgood and Morley make this process overt in that they assume unlike Stecher that the funds spend on the library would *not* be better spent elsewhere *and* that these funds are also spent in the most effective way. They contrast this with that of the operational researcher who "generally starts by asking 'What do you want to do?' and then sets about finding the most efficient way to do it. Inverse programming assumes that what is being done is being done efficiently and then says 'This is what you seem to want. Is this really the case?'

"The blend of activities that the library *is* producing is observed and compared with the various alternative blends that *could* be produced. The fact that one blend is chosen in preference to others implies that the value of the outputs are weighted in a certain way. The policy-makers are then presented with the weights that are found and asked if they agree. If they revise the implied weights to a significant degree, this suggests that a change in the blend of outputs would be preferred. The approach has a number of advantages. It is the only approach known to us which fits in with the existing decision structure. It conveys information concisely since it classifies and quantifies activities in a way relevant to decisions but also weights the activities".

Thus in their Durham studies they express the relative importance of each service in terms of the amount of it that would be of equivalent importance to the addition of one item of book stock. They concluded in their study of the Durham University library that:

1 item of new stock was worth the same as
4.6 items on inter-library loan, or
1300 user reference hours, or
90 items on long loan, or
200 items on short loan, or
3.3 hours of senior advice, or
9.1 hours of junior advice.

The model that they developed therefore makes explicit the qualitative maximising criterion which the university library manager uses and, by employing sensitivity analysis, ie, what would happen if the resources were allocated differently, policy options can be reviewed and the likely impact of changes in the resource mix more easily evaluated.

This model has been further refined by Hawgood and Morris in their study of Derbyshire County Libraries where policy options and likely benefits are reviewed by the different groups that are affected by the decision. These include the public, library staff, library users, ratepayers, and the library committee. There are two major weaknesses of this approach in that (1) it it assumed that there is a correlation between what a particular group perceives as benefit and actual benefit without providing any evidence to support the correlation, (2) the panels established to weight the policy options consisted of library staff acting as members of the public who would not necessarily be able to reflect accurately benefit perceptions held by the general public.

Libraries as Hawgood and Morley assert are complicated systems where nearly everything interacts with everything else. There are certain physical resources and a fixed budget. Each activity uses several resources and each research contributes to several activities. Thus the problem of the efficient allocation of library resources is a complex one and undoubtedly a significant contribution has been made here to the whole area of better resource management.

However the model does not shed any light on how well the library is meeting user needs as the whole emphasis is on library inputs in which it is assumed that certain outputs are achieved. It has therefore much in common with the approach of Morris Hamburg and his co-workers who claim that "inherent in the governmental decision to invest in library services is a decision to forego alternative governmental investments and such non-governmental use of funds as private investment and consumption. The benefits of governmental expenditure are expected to exceed costs, to the extent that the resources utilized would result in benefits which exceed costs in the private sector. Since funds can be invested in the private sector with an average rate of return of 10—15% governmental benefits are expected to exceed costs by this rate".

This study however takes the view that an attempt to establish a methodology to ascertain what benefits are being achieved should be undertaken before it can be accepted that these investment returns or inverted benefits are being realised.

Expected value of perfect information
Another attempt to relate returns on capital to library/information decisions has been made by Wills and Christopher. They introduced the concept of the expected value of perfect information (EVPI) and this is calculated for a new product marketing launch (although presumably it could be equally applied to other investment projects) by correlating a range of likely market shares with expected net pay-offs and by using Bayesian statistics, the probability of achieving a particular share is calculated. (EVPI was a concept originally developed by Professor Lindley on which the Wills and Christopher work is based). From this data it is possible to calculate the maximum that should be spent on information and rightly the authors define information not in narrow documentary terms, but to

include all the information that is required and thus will include for example the cost of market surveys.

There are a number of difficulties with this approach:

1 records would have to maintained in the library to relate the service given to the project, to which it is to be charged; and a particular problem here is the high volume of transactions that take place in many libraries;

2 it only indicates the maximum that can be spent on information in its wider sense and does not indicate how much specifically should be spent on documentary information or how the funds should be allocated once the library allocation is established;

3 in order for a library to be effective it needs to maintain some continuity in terms of acquiring and recording information in terms of anticipated requirements, so that there would still remain the question of how much should be allocated to the library for this generalised documentary role which could not be determined by the Wills and Christopher approach.

Finally, even assuming these difficulties can be overcome it does not provide a method by which the contribution of documentary information can be assessed in terms of the financial success of the project.

Document exposure

Hamburg et al (1974) regard the key university and public library objective as "exposure of individuals to documents of recorded human experience". As has been indicated previously a special library certainly does not exist to maximise exposure, but to maximise the impact that library information has on corporate goal achievement which may involve reducing or eliminating some exposures. Hamburg et al and Meier before them developed a number of different ways of calculating document exposure and these are correlated with specific input costs. Then again assuming standard private sector investment returns, the return on each exposure in dollars can be calculated. There are three basic methods of calculating document exposure (1) total library usage, ie, loans, renewals and inhouse use (2) item use days; this measure differs from that of counting exposures because it multiplies exposure by number of days borrowed (3) actual exposure times calculated by asking the user either to indicate days on which books are used or actual amount of time during the loan period spent on reading the borrowed item.

Lancaster (1977) identifies two major weaknesses of document exposure:

1 A book borrowed for five days is not necessarily used for five days or, indeed, used at all. This can only be determined by interviewing users, or a sample of users, at the time they return materials to the library — a difficult and time-consuming process. Also, the accuracy of the measures thus made is entirely dependent upon the accuracy of the users in remembering how much use they made of a particular publication. This problem may be avoided by sampling, to determine the average number of use days per circulation, and using this estimate as the basis for all item-use calculations of material used away from the library.

2 Events that should be considered approximately equal in value may be weighted differently. For example, a document used for one hour on each of five days counts as five item-use days, while the same document used for five hours in one day counts as only one item-use day.

Data based on questioning users clearly then is of doubtful reliability where user recall may be poor. Equally unreliable however are the unobtrusive measures employed by Politz, who glued pages together and checked whether the page seals had been broken; and Voos, who even more bizarrely and certainly not unobtrusively suggested taking fingerprints from pages. Ford (1973) and Hindle have both suggested that the amount of exposure in relation to loan retention periods may be very low indeed.

Exposure data in any case is entirely quantitative in that as Hamburg et al admit each exposure is assumed to confer the same benefit on the library user although presumably it would be possible to weight exposures on the basis of the type of material lent. The problem here is that benefits would be assumed whilst a preferable approach rejected by Hamburg et al would appear to be to attempt to establish a sample of actual benefits from which generalisations could be drawn.

Time saved and external comparison studies

Mason, Magson, Kramer, and K C Rosenberg have all

produced data justifying the existence of an inhouse library on the basis of the amount of user time that is saved by maintaining such a service. Mason for example indicated that the savings were of the order of £1 per quick reference to £20 for a literature search. Doctor Lewis, in the reported discussion on the Mason approach, makes the point that many information problems are tackled by scientific staff in their marginal time and may not therefore be a true saving in the sense that it is being used by Mason. This objection underlines the point made earlier by Frost that small time savings cannot necessarily be linearly aggregated, as there is evidence to suggest that short time savings are relatively worthless. It is also frequently assumed in these studies, as has again been stated previously, that all information supplied by the in house library is relevant to the work of the host organisation without providing any evidence to support that assumption. One further weakness of these studies is that the time penalties incurred by the user in making use of the library are often ignored.

There are further unresolved methodological difficulties in that both Kramer and K C Rosenberg asked users how much time they believed library use had saved them. There is however no way that a user can satisfactorily answer this question especially when it is frequently posed in general terms rather than relating the time savings to a specific use by the library. An attempt was made by Blagden (June 1975) to overcome the problem of unreliable user estimates of time saved, by attempting to simulate the conditions that would prevail in the libraryless organisation, by taking a sample of already answered, timed, information requests and comparing the time taken to answer these requests using external sources. The time taken and the quality of answers obtained were then compared with the original times and original quality of the answers.

As far as speed was concerned the study demonstrated that the in-house library located information five times more quickly than the user working in an organization without a library. In addition the quality of answers obtained by the in-house library was generally far superior to those answers obtained by the user without a library.

The data[1] collected in this study cannot be regarded as reliable, because it was limited to only eight external searches although this involved the surrogate user in some six days of external search effort. Employing a surrogate user as opposed to the actual user is a further weakness of this approach as Swanson has pointed out "since many people have different interests and values, different reasons for them and different purposes and orientations, it is impossible for one person to fully substitute for another."

In the review of the Allen studies we were discussing the performance of literature where it was unknown as to whether this was supplied by a library or not. It is important here to make the performance assessment distinction, that we are concerned, as a profession, with isolating the beneficial role of libraries in transferring information, and we have to recognize that we are only one agency at work here. We have therefore to demonstrate not only the value of published information, but the value that a library *adds* to this process as the GLC study crudely shows in terms of speed of supply and quality of answer.

The attempt by Blagden was a step towards what is frequently asserted as the ideal library evaluation of comparing a group of users who have access to an in-house library and a matching control group who would be deprived of such a facility. Both the administrative difficulty of implementing this and the problem of establishing a matching control group would appear however to eliminate this as a viable approach.

King and Bryant do however believe that the theme of alternatives to the library can be pursued when they state that "usually there are other means of obtaining similar services for which the price can be readily determined and this can be used by the managing body as a frame of reference for arriving at an appropriate price for the in-house service." Lancaster (1971) lists the comparative criteria for making the in-house or buy out decision: (1) cost (Martyn and Vickery expand this into cost of operation and ease of set-up) (2) recall (3) precision (4) response time (5) user effort. As the use of external computerised

---

[1] Despite these limitations the data was used extensively by senior management not only to justify the library service, but also other technical support functions where it was assumed that the factor of five efficiency ratio would still apply.

information bases grows so the criteria outlined above will become more readily applied on a comparative basis with the in-house effort required to produce a similar service. A difficulty with this approach is that rarely will outside agencies be able to offer the complete range of services provided by the in-house service and thus the analysis will be of a piecemeal nature.

Magson did however attempt to conduct a complete information service evaluation and approached the problem of simulating the libraryless environment by asking how, and where at present is information collected and how and from where at present is information collected and how and from where it would be collected in the absence of a library. He then compared the costs of providing information on both an in-house basis, and by using external sources, although it was not clear how these external costs were determined. He identified three alternatives to the library (1) external commercial services by spot contract (ii) suitable nominees within the company, eg secretaries (3) nobody, ie users would obtain information directly from the best sources on a need-to-know basis. Magson worked on the basis that all library activities are essential in the first place otherwise they would not be carried out. Time saved data is usually employed to convince managers outside the library, who are responsible for funding, of the value of the service. The assumption that all library activities are essential would I suspect be hotly disputed by many of these, which could make the whole exercise counterproductive. It would seem preferable therefore to provide some evidence at the outset demonstrating the essential nature of these library activities. However if you have managed to do that there may no longer be any requirement for the time-saved, justificatory data!

Time-saved and external comparison studies clearly can provide data which can be used as a justification for an in-house service. However as Swanson indicates, there are three major options open to library managers once an evaluation has taken place: (1) discontinue service (2) restructure service (3) retain it as it is. Frequently data collected in these type of studies will tend to favour option (3) because most libraries will be able to demonstrate significant time savings by maintaining an in-house service. This assumes of course that one is able to either ignore or overcome the methodological problems outlined in this section.

The Edinburgh studies
The object of this study by Professor Wolfe and his co-workers was to develop a general methodology for the evaluation of services provided within a government department or business enterprise when the service is not sold at a price that covers its cost. In particular they studied the provision of non-primary information, ie, abstract journals, title listings, selective dissemination of information and inquiry answering.

Like many investigators Wolfe et al were very frank about the weakness of the approach that they finally selected. They assumed that the research production function had the following form:

$$R = f(S, I)$$
$$S = E + N$$

where R = Research Output
S = Scientific Input
I = Secondary information input
N = Information activity among scientific personnel
E = Scientific research activity of such personnel.

They reject the possibility, at least in the investigation, that an increase in I will reduce the efficiency of E activity by causing a diversion of effort into wasteful activities. They assume that scientists optimise their reading activities and will not read more than is necessary. All the work on relevance would not, however, appear to lend much support to that assumption. They admit that no evidence is offered for the proposition that research output depends in a proportional fashion upon numbers of hours taken by each worker and admit that if a logarithmic relationship applied this would have seriously affected their numerical results.

Although this was a cost benefit study, the criteria used to evaluate the performance of the technical information systems studied by Wolfe was again the value of time saved by using secondary information services rather than the value of the information itself. The measure was based on the assumption that the user of information would have to increase the amount of time searching for information and reading, if secondary services were not available to him.

The data was collected by structured interview from a sample of research workers, librarians and budget allocators or research directors. Again Wolfe is his own best critic when he states "one of our measures depends upon the subjective estimates of certain objective facts, ie, the effect of less information work upon research output". They also admitted that there was no definite relationship between the subjective assignment of value to a service and the valuation as observed from actual choice.

The time-saved data was obtained by asking scientists:

"Compare the present situation, in which you and your colleagues have access to secondary information services, with the hypothetical situation in which none of these is available. You may then choose to spend some extra time in doing your own information search, or you may choose to adjust to the situation in some other way.

"Please indicate the changes you would make in the number of hours you would devote to:
1 research and development work
2 information search
3 other work
Please indicate the weekly average number of hours worked."

Scientists responding, generally stated that they would reduce their research effort and spend more time on searching for information. The value of these information services was taken to be reflected in this time that would be taken by researchers on this additional search effort in the absence of secondary information services. As this was a cost benefit study this time was converted into money by assuming that if 10% of a scientist's time was spent on information work in the absence of these secondary services then this would reduce research productivity by 10%. This 10% figure was then equated with the scientists salary, so that if he was earning £3,500 per annum the benefit derived from having these information services would be calculated as £350. This is of course very similar to the way in which the time saved money values were calculated in the previous section.

Wolfe also employed a form of shadow pricing to obtain some of his data, ie, by getting the R & D worker to distribute 100 points between services. However, subjective assessments of this sort are based on utility analysis which Wessell also employed in his investigations. Again it depends on the concept that the consumer not only knows that he prefers A to B, but he can give numerical expression to his desires which permits him to say he prefers A say twice as much as B. Here we must requote Wolfe himself "economists have in the past been reluctant to rely upon surveys of consumers' expressed preferences. I am mainly inclined to the view that only choice revealed in the market could offer evidence about consumers' underlying preferences". However, few special libraries are directly in the market place and this is where many of the problems of adapting the tools of the economists arise.

Wolfe also indicates a further ambiguity in dividing one hundred points between two alternative modes of service. The ambiguity arises in terms of whether the division is either to be based on consumer surplus[1] ie, what is the maximum that a consumer would pay for a particular product, or on the marginal rate of substitution, ie, at what point will one cease purchasing one product and start buying a substitute product.

The results of the study would appear to indicate that secondary information must almost always score the highest value as compared with trade literature, personal inside contacts and personal outside contacts. This is true of the five industries surveyed[2] in the study except for engineering, where trade literature achieved the highest score. This appears to conflict with the results obtained by Allen, but it is worth re-emphasising that Allen based his conclusions on an analysis of significant messages received for a specific research project, whilst Wolfe's conclusions are based on generalised subjective estimates of value. Nevertheless, the Wolfe study was based on a large sample (93 firms) and provides a wealth of data on user attitudes which would not appear to have had as much impact on the library

[1] Consumer surplus is the difference between the actual price consumers pay and the maximum that they are willing to pay.
[2] The other four were agriculture, chemicals, aircraft and textiles.

profession as they perhaps should have done (for example the low value assigned to users to enquiry answering services and the high rating given to abstract publications). This study then has provided a large amount of data on users' perception of the utility of information and data on the costs of information provision. However, because the focus of the study was based on user perceptions of time saved, the data so derived is subject to the same criticisms as those already made earlier.

The Wessel studies
Wessel and his co-workers attempted to develop criteria for evaluating a number of United States Army technical libraries, and in so doing developed a range of evaluative techniques, two of which are reviewed in this section.

1 *Score* (Service, Components, Reliability and Efficiency Analysis) is a systematic procedure for identifying the costs and degree of success of various library functions. When this data is collected the technique can be used to forecast the probability of success and the effect that changes in the library system mix can have on the future success rates. The analysis is based therefore on demand so that if for example all 200 enquiries examined in the analysis were answered by the deadline, then the timeliness effectiveness achieved by the information service would be 100%. How satisfactory the answers were, would provide another measure and so on.

The difficulties of who is to judge success and from what viewpoint do not however appear to be satisfactorily resolved by the Score approach. In addition Score's effectiveness indexes are limited to demand rather than need although Wessel et al do attempt to establish whether demand does fall within a particular library's 'mission statement'. Another problem is that it is assumed that all contacts with the library have an equal value and the technique did not weight the success rates even by the perceived value of the user.

2 *Scout* (Service, Components, Utility Analysis) is based on the library manager assigning an estimated utility value representing the relative contribution that each library operation is making towards user needs. This is correlated with how much input is being put into each operation

relative to the total resources available to the library manager. Wessel found that the library managers' judgement of utility was usually consistent with the way he had allocated his budget.

As with Score no evidence is presented to demonstrate that there is a relationship between a librarian's utility estimates and corporate contribution: a similar conclusion to the one that was reached in the section on benefit inversion.

The first half of this book has attempted to present a critical review of the conceptual background to the problem of evaluating a library's performance together with specific comment on the approaches and techniques that are available to the evaluator. In addition a review has also been presented of significant studies relevant to this investigation in which it has been demonstrated that our knowledge of what contribution libraries in general and special libraries in particular make, towards corporate goals is extremely limited.

Earlier it was stated that the purpose of this particular evaluative study was to establish how far a library system was falling short of the ideal system described by King and Palmour "which would permit every message to be transmitted only to the recipients who will use the information when the information is required and at a cost that is less than or equal to the value of the information!" It has now been concluded however that the approach of attempting to put a money value on the information supplied is not a viable approach. The original aim of this study is modified therefore to establish the value of the system not in monetary terms but the degree to which the system contributes to corporate goals.

The focus of the fieldwork described in chapters six and seven will be to establish whether information distributed by the two libraries benefited the organisations that they are serving. It is the approach embodied in the question posed by Menzel in the context of scientific information when he asks "What services can the science information system perform that will contribute to the research productivity of that body of scientific researchers? The formulation of the question immediately calls for a qualitative categorisation of functions of the information system. Only then is it possible to state that the performance of some of these functions is needed in a given situation and that of others is not needed, or that some are needed more, some less". Menzel goes on to define the requirements of such a system:

1 an information system containing mechanism, ie, the media of communication;

2 which will deliver to each scientist messages of certain (1) format (2) content (3) points of origin (eg, age, language, etc);

3 in response to directives of a certain permanence and a certain scope of coverage (eg, current awareness or enquiry answering services);

4 so as to result in certain changes in the scientist's cognitive state.

5 which will lead to decisions about issues.

Section four of the Menzel framework is further elaborated by Hatt who outlines the various exit patterns from the reading act:

i. reader perception of the text
ii. reader decodes the text
iii. reader accepts the message
iv. reader uses message to confirm an attitude or opinion
v. reader retains message
vi. reader makes a decision on the basis of the message.

This is a condensed simplified version of the eleven exit patterns identified by Hatt to which reference has already been made and at almost any state the message can be either discarded or distorted. It also assumes that the message itself is clear.

Of course, this is only part of the classic communication model — who, why, when, where, how, to whom, with what effect — to which reference has also already been made and as Saracevic puts it, one really needs to establish whether the signals were received as sent, whether the meaning was understood in the same way, and whether the desired outcome was achieved.

It would appear that library evaluation has not as yet even established whether the signals were received, yet alone whether the meaning was understood by the recipient in the same way as the sender. If the reader both decodes the text and accepts the message is it always clear what the message was anyway, especially when he simply uses the library documentation to confirm an attitude or an opinion? If the reader rejects the message can this be fairly construed as a failure on the part of the library or should it not be regarded as a benefit in that it established that that particular line of enquiry should no longer be pursued.

Special libraries exist to provide information which can be used to take a decision. As Murdoch and Liston point out: "many people will argue that knowledge as defined here has no intrinsic value; that only when it is successfully transferred can its value be realised. Others go further arguing that the value of information cannot be realised unless it is actively applied in decision making". Is it legitimate, however, to ignore the cognitive enrichment of individual readers that a special library achieves through the distribution of documentation, if it does not at that *time* result in any action? Even if action does take place it is still not sufficient to stop the evaluative process even at this point, because it then has to be established how good that decision was and here the Allen approach of the super judge would appear to be worth pursuing. Over what time scale should the evaluation take place and how are the measures developed from the impact that library documentation makes going to be related to the total information universe.

It is planned in the fieldwork to attempt to shed some light on these questions and to introduce two new evaluative approaches to the problem of evaluating library performance.

Essentially the approach is one of evaluating the interaction between the library and the user in terms of the specific document or information that is supplied to that user. It is therefore complementary to the approach of Thomas Allen in that instead of recording significant messages and relating these to performance, the proposed approach will examine specific library 'messages' and attempt to ascertain what contribution they make to the parent organisation. Of course this approach can be subjected to the same criticism that Fabisoff and Ely make that studies of information needs should concentrate on needs rather than the system supplying that need. However hopefully this problem will be reduced by focussing on corporate contribution and by also attempting to set the use of the library in the context of total information universe to which the library user is exposed.

Penetration is the first stage of the evaluative process to be used in the fieldwork in which one is simply attempting to determine how well the messages are getting through to the audience to whom they are aimed. In attempting to establish such data one has to divide the audience into homogeneous segments as clearly different groups will have differing information needs.

Impact moves into the area of cognitive enrichment which Childers regards as the most difficult area to measure. Impact anlaysis, in the context of the fieldwork described will attempt to determine whether the messages have been received, ie read and what outcomes resulted from this reading. It will result in the establishment of a library impact mix and the library manager can then decide if this particular mix is the one best suited to the needs of the host organisation. Impact does not therefore assume that all library use is beneficial or confers equal benefits and that the library manager's role is to maximise corporate contribution not necessarily library use, unless they are in complete harmony.

Cawkell similarly points out that since the action a user takes can vary from a decision that an article is obviously relevant and should be filed for future reference, to an immediate change in a research project, then obviously there are degrees of action and impact analysis will attempt to establish these degrees. It is the alternative research strategy used by Rosenbloom and Wolek who concentrate on the impact of information on the job as opposed to restricting it to impact on the user. It is also planned to concentrate like Wolek and Rosenbloom on ways in which information is of value rather than direct measures of such value.

It has also much in common with the approach that Greenberg and Mattison adopted in their evaluation of health education literature which is illustrated overleaf.

Suchman distinguishes between penetration, which he calls effectiveness, and impact, in a similar way:
"By the latter term I mean the strength of influence

Number or proportion of persons who are meeting prescribed and accepted standards
Number or proportion of persons who change their patterns of behaviour in accordance with the new knowledge. This may be verbalized but is more accurate when observed in action
Number or proportion of persons who change opinions or attitudes from the new knowledge
Number or proportion of persons who learn the facts contained therein
Number or proportion of persons who glance at or read it
Number or proportion of persons who see the material
Number or proportion of persons who receive the material
Number of requests received for the material, or number distributed
Number of pieces of literature available for distribution
Pretesting of literature by special readability formulas.

upon exposed individuals. A programme or activity may have considerable impact affecting markedly the thoughts and actions of those it touches; it will necessarily be judged ineffective if it is so designed that this impact is confined to a small fraction of the group it is intended to reach and influence".

The fieldwork therefore will be based on the premise that attempts to evaluate the use made of a special library is a fruitful line of enquiry and differ with the conclusion reached by Haney, Harris and Tipton who assert that:

1 the first, and most immediate, conclusion to be drawn relative to the impact of print on adult behaviour is that it is generally unimpressive and almost always unpredictable;

2 studies demonstrate that adult behaviour is rarely

altered by the printed word and that indeed most adults read (purposefully) in order to reinforce already existing attitudes and opinions.

SIX

ASSESSING A CONSTRUCTION DESIGN LIBRARY BY MARKET PENETRATION AND IMPACT CRITERIA

THE FIELDWORK reported in the next two chapters attempts to apply the evaluative concepts of market penetration and impact in two libraries. The two studies took place at the Greater London Council (GLC) and the British Institute of Management (BIM). They have been presented separately as the GLC study can in many ways be regarded as an extensive pilot for the BIM investigation. Under each study an outline is presented of the organization that the library is serving; a description of the library; a review of relevant studies of the client groups that the libraries are serving; a description of these client groups; an outline of the study; and the key results, particularly those that give an insight into the methodological strengths and weaknesses of this approach to library assessment. It is worth emphasizing that these two chapters are only a summary of the two investigations and those interested in the more detailed results should consult the original thesis on which this book is based. In addition much information contained in the BIM study was not included in the thesis or this book because it was not directly relevant to the search for an effective library performance assessment methodology. This omitted data includes detailed lists of the most popular journals/newspapers read by managers; the amount of time they perceive as spending on reading published information; the sources from which these publications were obtained and the names of the specific organisations contacted by managers when seeking information from outside the firm. This additional material has recently been jointly published in 1980 by the Cranfield Institute of Technology Press and the British Institute of Management entitled *"Do Managers Read"*?

THE GLC STUDY

The organisation
The Greater London Council came into being in 1964 and started operations in 1965 providing services which affect Greater London as a whole. It is the largest local authority in the country employing some 120,000 staff and with an annual budget of £1,940m. It covers an area of 611 square miles in which over 7 million Londoners live. It is in conjunction with the London Boroughs responsible for a wide range of functions including regional planning, metropolitan roads, traffic management, regional parks, refuse disposal, building control in Inner London, recreation and the arts, London Transport, Thames flood prevention, fire authority, education in Inner London only and housing.

This study is restricted however to one of the departments in the GLC namely the Architects Department which employed in 1977 over 3,050 personnel. The department is responsible for the design, construction, alteration and maintenance of nearly all the Council's and Inner London Education Authority's building. Gathered under its mantle is almost every service connected with building. Besides architects and technicians there are civil and structural engineers, building and quantity surveyors, specialists in landscape design and historic buildings, and a large schools maintenance organisation. The main bulk of the work of the department is devoted to the design and supervision of the building of new housing, schools, office buildings, court houses, ambulance stations and fire stations. It is also responsible for the rehabilitation and modernisation of existing buildings as well as preserving and restoring historic buildings. The department, in conjunction with the District Surveyor's service (which the library also serves), is responsible for the enforcement of the London Building Acts.

The overall objective of the design activities of the department have been stated as:

1 to carry out the new construction, improvement and maintenance work required by the Council and Authority

in accordance with programmes and briefs agreed with client departments;

2 to achieve the highest possible standards of architectural and technical quality within the financial and other constraints which are imposed; to achieve the greatest possible value for money both in the work done and in the use of resources;

3 to safeguard the interests of the public, through the control of the safety of buildings and structures and the preservation of historic buildings.

Access[1]

Access: the library information service consisted of 20 staff with a total budget of around £150,000 per annum (as at 1977) of which approximately £40,000 was spent on acquisitions. As has already been indicated the service primarily focuses on the provision of technical documentary information in support of the design and other activities that provide input to the Council's building programme. The library is a central source for all publications and as it serves some 100 different locations over a 600 square mile area, many publications are supplied to these subsidiary locations on a permanent basis. The central services does provide an enquiry answering and document supply facility as well as an extensive product information service.

In addition in the central facility there is a large building product sample collection, and a library of 'bricks' so that Access is not restricted to the dissemination of documentary information and is now also responsible for the systematic collection and recording of design experience.

Previous studies

Architects, engineers and quantity surveyors at the GLC are there to produce functional building designs and as Vickery (1973) states "he needs information on any subject that will contribute to his design but it must be available in readily applicable form since he works to a schedule and cannot afford to spend much time on the search".

However Gerstberger and Allen are convinced that engineers select information channels in a manner which is

[1] Architects Central Constructional Engineering Surveying Service.

intended to minimise loss, ie keeping to a minimum physical or psychological effort. Orr however argues that there could be exceptions to this "in that for many information needs only a small amount of good information is required and that such undemanding requirements can be therefore answered by any communication channel". Wolek too suggests that when engineers face needs which involve complex messages they turn to literature and Disch maintains that engineers face such time pressures that they select sources that yield information in the shortest space of time. The North American Aviation study conversely indicates that when there is more time available for a task, the task worker makes heavier demands for information.

What does however appear to be undisputed are the conclusions resulting from the Gralewska-Vickery study of earth science engineers in that published information is only a small part of the total information to which engineers are exposed and that the predominant mode of communication is oral. Most studies would also appear to support Hanson in that engineers appear to use documentary information much less than scientists. However, as he points out there are a number of possible explanations for this: (1) the practice of engineering generates less information (2) or engineering depends less on information than does science or (3) engineering information is less well organised than science.

Calder suggests another reason for this light use when he suggests that the less scientific a matter is and the closer it comes to normal work, the less the technologist apparently expects to learn about it from literature, (a point confirmed in another later extensive survey conducted by Wolek and Rosenbloom).

It is against this background of comparatively light use of documentary information by which the GLC study should be judged.

The target groups
Access, aims its services at a wide range of constructional professionals including mechanical, electrical, civil, and structural engineers, quantity surveyors, building surveyors and architects.

Mechanical and electrical engineers are however served by an outlier library and as the study was conducted at the central library, mechanical and electrical engineers have not been included. Similarly building surveyors who are also served by outlier facilities have also been excluded from the study.

This section therefore is restricted to reviewing studies of the information requirements of architects, civil engineers, structural engineers and quantity surveyors, engaged in the design process.

Architects
Bishop and Alsop define design as "those functions that use scientific principles, technical information and imagination to define a project capable of meeting specified requirements with economy and efficiency . . . as design progresses there is a continuing need for information of many kinds. Some of this is peculiar to the project, perhaps contained in the brief or site survey or in drawings, schedules or specifications. Much of the information is more general being drawn either from the conspectus of knowledge or from the information structured to inform designers of the past performance of projects, functional systems or building elements or from information about materials, products and components".

A Department of Environment study also makes the distinction between project information, eg, the client's brief, production drawings, correspondence and calculations, and general information, eg codes of practice, building regulations and research reports. The Department of Environment report however adds a third category on organisational information, eg standard details and costs and other job output data.

In the table shown overleaf reproduced from Goodey & Mathew the main sources of technical information are illustrated and it is significant to note the high emphasis given to information emanating from building product manufacturers.

Roberts and Snow both confirm that architects spend relatively little of their time on published information. It is to be expected that the 538 GLC architects which the central library is serving will conform to this pattern. The

Table 4 What are your main sources of technical information?

		%
Trade reps visiting your office	249	59
Courses	25	6
Films	37	9
Literature (Trade)	382	90
Literature (Research establishments)	243	57
Journals/Magazines	359	85
Trade exhibitions	72	17
Building & Design Centres	155	37
Telephoning or writing to manufacturers	302	71
Telephoning or writing to research establishments	117	28

538 figure includes trainees, technicians, and qualified architects. The information that this group of architects will require will mainly be limited to the public sector buildings for which the GLC has responsibilities.

Civil Engineers
A Ministry of Public Building and Works paper summarising the report prepared on its behalf by Freeman Fox identified the key areas in which the civil engineer is interested as highways, railways, bridges, tunnels, airfields, pipelines, ports, harbours and sea defence works, water supply, drainage, sewage disposal, hydro-electric schemes and dams, thermal power stations and heavy foundations. The same report also maintains that soil mechanics is of paramount interest to the civil engineer. The main constituents of which are (1) site investigations, bore holes, in situ tests, geophysical surveys, (2) laboratory tests on samples, (3) interpretation of tests, (4) soil testing during construction, (5) soil stress conditions, (6) soil stabilisation. The report concludes that the development and systems for the rapid retrieval of information on similar engineering projects giving details of local costs, resources and natural conditions should be given priority.

The GLC Civil Engineers working in the Architects Department do have a narrower information requirement than that described above in that their civil engineering activities are almost entirely in support of a new housing work. They generally therefore do not get involved in substantial constructions, eg, motorways and large bridges, but focus on housing estate roads, pedestrian footbridges and subways and other smaller types of construction.

The number of Civil Engineers in the two main complexes served by the central library total 129 which again includes technicians and trainees.

Structural Engineers
A structural engineer's role is usually confirmed to the structural design of a building and its foundations to ensure that the building is safe under the probable combinations of loading which occur. In the context of the GLC this can be further amplified to include geotechnics, structural design and properties of materials. In addition to the structuring engineering work undertaken by the GLC structural engineers in the course of the department's building programme, there is also a section of the division which has statutory responsibilities under the London Building Acts.

Stevens and Monument divide structural engineering information into hard information, ie drawings, specifications, schedules of various kinds and soft, ie, speech and correspondence. However the same authors divide information more conventionally into project related information, ie, site and structural details and constraints and non-project information, ie, properties of materials and sections, methods of structural analysis, cost data and knowledge of building regulations. The number of structural engineers that the Central Service is attempting to serve including trainees totals 119.

Quantity Surveyors
It could be argued that the information requirements of the quantity surveyor are substantially different from those of the preceding target groups as quantity surveyors are not directly concerned with design. Drake however argues that the quantity surveyor working in the field of educational building (as many of GLC Quantity Surveyors do) needs to be as well informed as the architect on matters of educational philosophy. Farrar and Malthouse to some extent agree when they state that during the cost planning and cost checking processes the Quantity Surveyor is working in close collaboration with the designer throughout the various

stages of design. However they also point out that "in the production of Bills of Quantities and the checking and analysis of tenders he is working in comparative isolation but hereafter his task of monetary control, valuations for interim payments and agreement of final accounts is performed in conjunction with the main contractor and nominated sub-contractors. His final cost analysis of the contract will provide the feed-back information to be used when the cycle of events is restarted for some future job'. This feed-back information is of course a vital part of the GLC Quantity Surveyors' information resource that is at his disposal. This is entirely separate from the library and information service.

Farrar and Malthouse also identify seven main routines of the Quantity Surveyor (1) cost planning (2) cost checking during design (3) production of Bills of Quantities (4) cost analysis of tender (5) valuation for interim payments (6) preparation of variation (final) account (7) cost analysis of the contract.

Study outline

The study's main aim was to establish how well product information distributed by Access was getting through to these construction professionals and what contribution this information made to the design process.

At the outset it was decided to limit the investigation to one part of the Access service namely an extensive file of manufacturers literature on building products relevant to the Council's building programme. There were two main reasons why this approach was adopted (1) product information can be regarded as primarily of a hard nature (hardness has already been defined in chapter one) and thus would not possibly give the measurement problems that perhaps more general information would present and (2) as this was essentially a pilot for a wider investigation there was no need to attempt to measure the impact of the whole service on the target audience.

Bishop and Alsop describe in some detail the process entailed in searching product information. The search process includes product identification, properties, dimensions, costs, application, availability, distribution and testing. Many commentators such as Wolfe et al and

R A Davis emphasize the importance of trade literature and more specifically Snow maintains that architects rely on trade literature as a major information source.

This high regard for trade literature is reflected in the data on the frequency of and the amount of time spent, in using this literature. R M S Hall maintains that one fifth of a designers time is spent searching for product information and that time spent on use has to be added to this total. Davis surveyed 1800 engineers and 85% of them used trade catalogues and over half of these used them weekly. Goodey and Mathew in a survey of 423 architects use of trade literature contained in office libraries indicate that daily use of trade literature appears to be the norm and significantly among local authorities participating in the Goodey and Mathew survey this was as high as 82%. Sutton too confirms in an extensive report on an engineering design study that 47% of respondents use trade literature daily. R M S Hall also stated that 50% of designers used trade literature daily.

The Access file contains information on approximately 10,000 products issued by over 2,000 manufacturers. It is arranged by CI/SFB and there is an index of trade names, an alphabetic index to the classification and a manufacturers index. There is however no classified catalogue but a reference copy of every leaflet is maintained on the shelf providing in practical terms such a facility. Evaluative information on these products which is also included in Access is separated from the product files and is excluded from this study. Each catalogue has however attached to it a 'traffic signal' sticker which does attempt to give an indication as to the performance of that product.

The service is not at present open access and library staff act as intermediaries between the system and the customer. The service cannot provide the kind of property data facility fully described by Dehlinger, eg, the service can identify and provide literature on aluminium sliding windows, but it cannot give any indication of comparative performance of this window with other windows except by simply comparing the statements made in the literature describing similar products. The service cannot answer such questions as 'is there a building component which has these properties which will give this type of performance'?

The study consisted of recording all interactions with the service over a four week period. This resulted in nearly 700 interactions being recorded and was hopefully sufficient data on which generalisation about the nature and patterns of use could be made.

Eighteeen interviews were conducted as well as five group discussion meetings and the information generated from this stage of the study provided the impact data.

Penetration calculations were based on the four week usage data (which included visit frequency data) in order to determine how well the service was going to reach the individual segmented groups (architects etc). In order to calculate the number of users expected in the next four week period the 1975 Brookes sampling theorem was employed, but that technique while reasonably accurate for one four week period to a second four week period, is nowhere near good enough for extrapolation to longer time spans. So the next calculation is to estimate the population P of 'susceptible' users, that is users who might be expected to use the system at one time or another. This gives P = 402 suggesting an overall (rather than annual) percentage penetration of 75% as shown in table five.

The actual calculation of P is somewhat complicated and here I am indebted to Dr S Robertson of the City University for the following explanation. First imagine that you are trying to estimate the population of fish in a lake. You catch a number S, mark them and turn them loose. Then you wait a few days and catch S again, of these A are unmarked. A simple probability calculation gives the total population

$$P = \frac{S^2}{S-A}$$

But this assumes that all fish are equally likely to be caught. In the Greater London Council's four week usage data frequent users are going to be more in evidence than the infrequent user[1] In other words a Pareto distribution applies here in that something like 20% of the population may account for as much as 80% of the usage. If therefore one is assessing penetration on the basis of

---

[1] Evans et al maintain that several studies have shown that a few active users account for a high proportion of total library usage.

numbers of *users* recorded using the service over a four week period, some account of this distribution has to be considered in the final calculation. The Greater London Council visit frequency data was therefore corrected by a later 1979 Brookes theorem, which attempts to take account of this.

In table five therefore the data is presented in terms of how many users the service will reach.

Table 5 Penetration analysis by numbers of personnel reached

	column 1 Numbers of Access users[1] in four weeks	column 2 Total target audience	column 3 Percentage penetration for four week period	column 4 Total percentage penetration
Architects	171	538	31.8	75
Quantity surveyors	44	263	16.7	25
Structural engineers	17	119	14.3	22
Civil engineers	18	129	14	64

[1] Design staff only

Column one lists the number of Access users in the four week period and data was also collected on frequency of use and number of queries posed per visit. Column two lists the total numbers of design staff that the service is attempting to reach and column three presents a single percentage penetration based on the data collected in the four week survey period. Column four presents the data corrected by the Brookes theorem and here the percentage rises considerably. However it would still appear that the service is only going to reach a disappointing proportion of the target audience ranging from 75% in the case of architects to less than 22% in the case of structural engineers.

Table six reworks the data by number of *requests* received during the four week period in contrast with table five which presented numbers of personnel using the service. These requests are then expressed as a percentage of the total expected incidence of product information decision making.

This assumes that architects require product information daily, an assumption based on the Goodey and Mathew survey to which reference has already been made. It has also been assumed that quantity surveyors need product

Table 6 Penetration analysis by number of contacts with service

	column 1 Number queries posed in survey period	column 2 Optimum incidence of product information decision-making over four weeks (job personnel only)	column 3 Percentage penetration for four week period	column 4 Annual number of queries likely to be posed	column 5 Annual optimum incidence of product decision-making	column 6 Annual percentage penetration
Architects	371	5557	6.7	4693	70296	6.7
Quantity surveyors	87	1014	8.6	1101	12827	8.7
Structural engineers	30	106	28.3	380	1338	28.3
Civil engineers	28	275	10.2	354	3485	10.2

Table 7 Penetration based on work activity (architects only)

column 1 Annual number of queries likely to be posed by Housing Architects	column 2 Number of jobs at two peak information gathering stages[1]	column 3 Number of jobs only at working drawing stage	column 4 Annual optimum incidence of decisions based on 351 total	column 5 Percentage penetration 351 total	column 6 Annual optimum incidence of decisions based on 138 total	column 7 Percentage penetration 138 total
2188	351	138	70902	3.1%	28876	7.6%

[1] Includes both jobs at the working drawing stage and those in construction.

information every two days, civil engineers every four days, and structural engineers every eight days. This is based on informed estimates in the absence of any data.

Column one presents the number of requests made by the target groups using the service and column two presents the number of product information decisions likely to be made during that four week period. However, because Access is open 253 days per year and staff only work 202 days, the figures in column two have been corrected to allow for this. The annualized data presented in columns three, four, and five give therefore the same penetrative figure as the four week data.

In table seven we introduce another factor in assessing penetration performance, namely the stage at which the design had reached as clearly this is likely to be an important factor in determining the need for product information.

The table is restricted to housing work because data on other parts of the Council's building programme was not readily available. Those schemes that were involved in preliminary feasibility studies were excluded as it was likely that architects engaged on schemes at this stage would have little or no need for product information. They would probably be relying at this stage on published information rather than specific proprietary literature.

Column one of table seven presents the annualized total of use of the service by housing architects based on the actual housing architectural usage of Access during the four week period. Column two lists the total of all housing schemes that were underway during the four week survey period which had completed the preliminary feasibility study. Column three lists the total of the schemes at the working drawing stage which is regarded as a peak product information gathering stage. Columns four and six present numbers of product information decisions likely to be made during the year. Column four is based on all schemes beyond the preliminary feasibility stage and column six is restricted to those at the working drawing stage. The totals in these two columns assume that the number of schemes will remain constant throughout the year and also assumes that each scheme will generate a product decision every working day.

Columns five and seven present simple percentage

penetration figures which are not markedly different from the penetration calculations presented in table six. None of the data presented in tables five, six and seven has been corrected to allow for seasonal variations in the use of the service.

The assumption on which the Access product information section operates is that for staff served by the central service, the service should always be used when the decision requires information from manufacturers' literature.

The reasons for this assumption are that (1) the time penalty to the user is very modest, (2) wrong decisions made on product selection can have a very high cost penalty and (3) the evidence obtained from studying the use of the collection would appear to indicate that the information required is almost always immediately available, (4) the use of this collection also enables the enquirer to a limited extent to also tap the mass of evaluative information maintained in the library on these products.

This assumption does mean therefore that the penetrative performance of Access would appear to be very poor indeed. However there are a number of organizational factors which will affect penetration although clearly it is not possible to introduce these as quantifiable input to the penetrative calculation. The key factors likely to affect penetrative performance are as follows:

1 In the last two decades heavy emphasis has been placed on standardisation within the department which has resulted in the use of repetitive designs for which the materials are pre-selected. This has taken a number of different forms:

i. almost all new housing work is designed from a restricted range of preferred dwelling types;

ii. the school building programme has been dominated by an industrialised system called MACE;

iii. every Job Architect is issued with a set of standard preambles; a document which specifies the performance required by the materials to be used and in a number of cases restricts the choice to named proprietary products;

iv. recently there has been a great deal of debate about the high incidence of building failures and there is now considerable pressure on design staff to use traditional products whose performance is well known rather than using new untested products;

2 Although product information is used very frequently it doesn't necessarily follow that each decision includes selection. What undoubtedly happens is that a product is identified, literature acquired, and at later stages in the design process this same piece of literature is examined to ascertain, for example, properties, dimensions and installation details.

3 In the public sector usually the jobs are designed on an entirely in-house basis which means that the Architect will make the initial decision on material choice and in many cases the Structural Engineer/Quantity Surveyor/Civil Engineer will obtain their information from the Architect.

4 There is also the problem of personal collections retained in the design group and the use that is made of these collections.

5 Design staff do have a great deal of direct contact with the manufacturers and their representatives.

6 Within the department there are other sources of information and advice on materials which again will affect the incidence of the use of the central collection.

7 The nature of the job would also affect the incidence of decision making about products. For a large job once a decision has been made about windows for example the need for product information on this category disappears. However proportionally the small job in terms of value of that job will make a larger number of product decisions.

Impact was established by interview and questioning users on information that they had borrowed and returned[1]. The items were borrowed in October/November but the interviews did not take place until late February early March of the following year. The interviewees were shown brochures that they had borrowed and were asked the questions shown below (this was only part of a wider ranging interview):

You recently approached Access for information on.... Can you tell me what this was for?
— What were you seeking to find out?

---

[1] By waiting until the borrowed item was returned it overcomes the problem raised by Lantz at what point in time should one determine whether a particular reference was read.

— Was Access the only source you tried. If not, what others?
— Of what use was the information contained in the brochure to you?
— Why?
— Was it used for a particular scheme. If so, which?
— Was the catalogue the one you originally wished to obtain from Access?
— If not, why did you choose an alternative?
— How did you come to select this particular item?
— Were you aware of any evaluative reports on the suitability of their product?

The technique appeared to be successful in that the interviewees were able to effectively recall the circumstances which involved the use of the Access service. A typical response from a job architect is summarised below:

This enquiry arose because the interviewee was designing a refuse transfer station. This station design was based on a prototype built 5 years ago. The present design for the GLC's Public Health Engineering Department is an updated version of the prototype.

The design calls for one of the room walls to be lined with a steel strip covered with enamel. The material used in the original design was produced by Richard Thomas and Baldwin, now part of the British Steel Corporation. A revamped version of this product was produced by BSC and consequently he went to Access to learn something of its properties, since he was proposing to use this or a similar material.

However both Stelvetite and all other materials had a 'red' (see next page for an explanation) assessment; consequently went to the materials information group for advice. After consultation with MIG he was able to write a specification for a sub-contractor.

He did not need to consult any other source than Access although the material was selected in consultation with MIG.

Only twelve impact statements were collected, so no generalisations can be made about the benefit disbenefit mix that Access was achieving. Nevertheless it is worth working through these statements to demonstrate how impact analysis would work with more representative data.

Out of the twelve impact statements that were collected in two cases the interviewee could not recall ever having borrowed the two items that he was shown. The interviewer concluded that this was a defensive attitude and from the conversation it appeared that these two items were borrowed for private design purposes. Whatever the actual explanation, clearly the Access benefit mix drops from a potential of 100% to 83% as the purpose of the service is neither to distribute information that is not read nor provide information in support of private design work. Three of the items were read but not used directly in support of the design process, one was used for current awareness purposes and the other two involved products which on examination were rejected. Current awareness and product rejection are clearly of some benefit but cannot be regarded as directly beneficial in terms of support to the design process. Beneficial impact can be said to have dropped to 58%.

The other seven products were all used in the design process but here we attempted to evaluate the quality of that decision. Almost all product literature filed in the Access service has a 'traffic signal' sticker affixed to it to indicate to the Access user the opinion of the Department on the performance of that product. Products coded green are ones which the GLC have used successfully over a long period and therefore it is the department's view that these are perfectly safe to specify. The other colours really represent various shades of doubt about a product's suitability but it is a little misleading to suggest that all products that are not graded green should not be used. However, working on that basis, ie assuming that all non-green graded products should not be used, the effectiveness of the Access system in terms of the quality of design decision, taken on the basis of literature distributed, drops to 42%. It is worth emphasizing that non-green products are in many cases perfectly satisfactory provided they are specified for the appropriate application. It has in any case always been policy within Access to maintain a comprehensive collection which would include dubious products because if they are not available credibility of the service is impaired and users will simply contact manufacturers direct.

It was not as has already been stated possible to adjust the penetrative date on the basis of those organizational factors previously identified. In addition although the estimates of the incidence of product based decisions are unreliable they would have to be reduced considerably for penetrative performance to be improved significantly. It would appear then that the only way to improve performance would be to increase the library's market share by stimulating greater use of the service.

However an aggressive marketing approach may not be in the best interests of the host organization, as the information channels should be seen as mutually supportive rather than competitive. Thus, penetrative data does not give any indication as to what the library's market share *should* be in a situation where all communication channels are performing optimally.

That said however we did have within Access, an extensive well indexed, up to date collection of product information, housed in an attractive accessible open plan environment with (according to the group discussions and interviews) a helpful and competent staff. The managerial inclination therefore would be still to promote the service as vigorously as possible to increase the market share.

Although penetration was apparently poor 95% of the users of the service did immediately receive information in response to their queries. What of course is not known is whether this was the right information or how much of this use was conditioned by what was available. However in Orr's terms, the Access product information service appeared to come perilously close to his definition of a perfect library which has everything immediately available.

The impact results in contrast with penetration were encouraging in that the literature that was borrowed from Access was mainly used in support of design work. The number of impacts collected however was so small that they clearly cannot be regarded as at all representative. It did appear also however that decisions taken on the basis of these borrowings were likely to be technically sound ones. However this is not altogether surprising as product information is of such a specific nature that it was unlikely to produce any impact surprises. More significantly in the context of this study it was encouraging to discover how effectively users were able to recall the information seeking process that led to their use of the library; simply by being shown the specific item that was borrowed even though several months had elapsed between the borrowing and the interview.

SEVEN

ASSESSING A MANAGEMENT LIBRARY BY MARKET PENETRATION AND IMPACT CRITERIA

Managers' information requirements and studies of management behaviour

A difficulty, not encountered in the GLC study is the apparent dichotomy between what management is supposed to embrace and what managers actually do. Fayol defined management in terms of the acronym POSDCORB, ie, planning, organising, staffing, directing, co-ordinating, reporting and budgeting. More recently, Brech has defined management as: "A social process, entailing responsibility for the effective and economical planning and regulation of the operations of an enterprise in fulfilment of a given purpose or task, such responsibility involving (1) judgment and decision in determining plans and in using data to control performance and progress against plans, and (2) the guidance, integration, motivation, supervision of the personnel composing the enterprise and carrying out its operations".

However as Braybrooke asserts these four words (used by Fayol) do not in fact describe the actual work of managers at all, they describe certain vague objectives of managerial work. They are just ways of indicating what we need to explain. This problem is compounded by the fact that the fieldwork takes place in an organization, a key role of which is to provide information about management which does not necessarily have a very direct connection with what managers actually do. In addition, according to Glover "formal documented kinds of information will still be needed but other types may be more in demand relative to it. Plans may have to be more flexible and less obviously long term in character. Personal creativity and flair will become paramount with the reflective mode being devalued". The evaluation of the British Institute of Management's Management Information Centre must be viewed in the context therefore of an audience who generally rely on informal and internal sources of information and who may also be sceptical or indifferent to many management techniques which according to some commentators have been disgracefully oversold. However one would expect that managers who join the Institute may be more inclined to capitalise on documented management knowledge than their non-member counterparts. Another problem is that information disseminated by the Institute will be 'soft' supportive information and therefore difficult to evaluate in terms of corporate contribution, in contrast to the GLC study.

Sweeney provides a useful description of the information required by an industrial firm and by inference the manager, again emphasising the apparently small part that management science[1] type information plays:

    high quality of knowledge of personnel recruited;
    up-dating of this knowledge;
    data on user/consumer needs;
    market infra-structure data, tariffs, transport, population, characteristics, competition, etc;
    new process technology, machinery, production and packaging systems;
    new product technology, materials, sub-components, design data standards;
    management information, cost production sales;
    monitoring techniques, quality control, maintenance;
    management techniques, decision analysis, operational research.

Similarly libraries are only seen as one source of many from which this information is derived, of which the following are examples:

    the educational and training system, the research and technical system, universities, institutes, laboratories;
    libraries and information centres, the market, the government and its agencies, internal data generation processes, computer and other data stores;

---

[1] Roughly the kind of information mainly distributed by the Management Information Centre

computing and supplying organisations;

the media will include internal reports and documents, internal meetings, discussions with colleagues, meetings and other forms of personal contact with scientists, suppliers, civil servants and other experts, courses, conferences and training programmes, public media, newspaper journals, radio and TV, telecommunication links, enquiry services such as consultancy information services and research projects.

Wilkinson divides a manager's information needs into strategic and tactical planning. Strategic planning deals with problems that generally are complex and irregular, that involve numerous internal environmental factors and have had broad scopes with respect to organisational units or activities. Information needed for making strategic planning decisions is therefore broad in scope, summarized in form and gathered from a wide variety of sources. Although largely qualitative in nature, such quantitative data as opportunity costs, incremental costs and long range forecasts of sales amounts are usually needed to show the impacts of the various alternatives upon the firm's overall profitability. Timeliness and accuracy of the information are relatively unimportant. Tactical planning is concerned with problems that are complex and more rhythmic, that have shorter range effects, and that are narrower in scope than strategic problems. Thus the scope of the needed information is narrow and shorter in range. Because of the short, regular cycles in tactical planning, the content of the information includes historical trends that serve as guides for forecasting future values. Strategic information will frequently be gathered from outside and will be obtained by *informal methods* rather than through the formal in-house management information system.

Aguilar, in a study of where top managers obtain information on the company's role in the outside environment, found that 50% of the information came from outside the company. However, only 29% of the total sample (around 200) of sources were formal sources, again supporting Wilkinson, so for strategic information there is still a heavy emphasis on personal contact and internal information is still a very important ingredient in the system mix.

It would appear then that tactical information inevitably

emanates from inside an organisation and that strategic information which is generally gathered from outside is mainly excluded from the range of services offered by the Institute according to the categories identified by Aguilar. In evaluating the effectiveness of information transfer in a management environment one is faced with exactly the same problem as that faced by all information seekers as Rappaport indicates "there will be numerous instances in which the additional information will not be worth the incremental costs. Indeed, in some cases it may not be worthwhile to obtain initial information to determine whether developing the main information is economically sound. The gross decision rule, which suggests that data collection and refinement be continued until marginal costs exceed marginal benefits to the decision maker, furnishes little practical guidance".

Andrus similarly in discussing the design of management information systems points out that "management is interested in information not for its own sake but rather for the benefits it may generate. Value is assigned to information according to the expected result of decisions based on that information, as opposed to results received without the information".

The problems too of relating individual performance to corporate goals (let alone isolating information inputs to that performance) are well summarised by Campbell et al:

"The measures must be over the long term not merely day-to-day or short term.

"Effective managerial job behaviour includes many actions, not just one. In fact, optimisation of resource allocation demands a myriad of complex and multi-facet information processing activities.

"No specification is made about the number of potential configurations of effective managerial actions. That is, different managers, utilising entirely different behavioural patterns might still accomplish the same, or very similar, levels of optimisation.

"Effective managerial behaviour must be measured in terms of what the manager himself does on the job to effect optimisation.

"Effective managerial behaviour, even though measured solely by what the manager himself does, is still subject to any number of causal variables, including not only the manager's qualities but also the nature of human, financial and material resources available to him, and to the rest of the organisation.

"The perceived effectiveness of a manager may be altered by the level of effectiveness of other managers as they, in turn, seek to optimise their own allocation of resources towards the maintenance of their own organisational units.

"Finally, any manager's actions can affect all organisational units for which he possesses either full or partial (shared) responsibility. His actions are typically directed towards optimal resource utilisation in many units, instead of just one, and measures of his level of managerial effectiveness should take account of the fact of his multiple membership in the many units."

Performance appraisal systems have been used to overcome the problems outlined by Campbell to evaluate the effectiveness of managers. The appraisal process consists of a manager and his superior setting job objectives which fulfil the following requirements:

1 they should be compatible with overall company plans;
2 they should represent sufficient challenge to the manager;
3 they should be attainable through the manager's own efforts;
4 they should be clearly defined as to the actual task necessary for accomplishing them;
5 they should include methods for estimating how well they have been accomplished.

However, as Campbell, et al point out, "what are the varieties or combinations of organisational circumstances, personal characteristics, and behaviour patterns that are likely to be perceived as effective managing. What do managers do that may lead to their perceived success or their perceived failure. What are the products and signs of effective managing"?

Performance rating systems that have been used quite widely to monitor managerial performance have failed, as Campbell and others again make clear: "The problem with global ratings is that they cover up so much. We cannot discern from a specific manager's standing in a rank list of several men whether his various rankers form their gestalts of him from job relevant or job irrelevant information. We cannot know with much certainty what portion of any such global impression may be based on actual managerial job behaviours or on contaminants such as physical bearing, friendliness, interpersonal savvy, etc which though constituting aspects of society's conception of desirable characteristics, may be related to none or only a limited number of actions involving resource allocation. In other words, global judgement does indeed reflect a common way of looking at success in our society and in business, but it yields little in terms of better understanding the way in which success in our society and in business is achieved or the job behavioural correlates contributing to it. Moreover, it yields no knowledge about a manager's differing levels of effectiveness in handling various resource allocation problems and thus tacitly ignores the complex and multi-faceted information processing requirements of his job."

As the focus of this study is on corporate contribution then clearly these difficulties of evaluating managerial performance have to be taken into account, although hopefully the approach of basing the assessment on specific library messages may reduce these problems somewhat. Another major problem is the one referred to earlier where Vickery maintained that information seekers can be grouped into three distinct categories: the scientist, the technologist, and the manager, all of which have significantly different requirements. The problem with managers is the one identified by Vickery and emphasised by Glover when he asserts that "differences between the character of decision making in science and management are that in the first case where the output consists of verifiable knowledge of phenomena, decision making is supposed to be a quintessentially controlled and rational kind of activity. If information is lacking then decision (assertions) will not be made". Glover contrasts this with managers where most information is private and insufficient, in which time is a crucial element, and thus a much higher degree of risk and personal judgement is present, making it more difficult to evaluate objectively how good a piece of information is. The concept too of satisficing, ie not searching for the best solution but ceasing to search as soon as a satisfactory solution is found, is clearly related to the difficulty of evaluating information in a management environment.

Table eight summarises the significant studies of manager's work activities and these as Glover points out have tended to concentrate on behaviour, rather than action or outputs. As with the studies of construction professionals, many of these managerial studies appear to be beset with methodological problems. For example there is the problem identified in one of the earliest studies by Carlson in which he showed that "there were highly significant differences between what respondents said they did, what respondents appeared to think that they did and what they actually did".

The conclusions of Stewart (1976) are not however in dispute: "A characteristic of most management jobs, as shown by a number of studies, is a highly fragmented work pattern. Managers typically switch their attention every few minutes from one person or subject to another, although the frequency with which this happens will vary, both with the job and with the individual style of working. An observation study of retail chain store managers showed that over 40% of their activity took less than one minute." In the words of Fores and Glover, "managers are constantly disturbed from scheduled tasks and they appear to like it. They are not reflective planners but adaptable information manipulators who prefer live concrete situations. Another key conclusion made by Stewart (1967), in her earlier work, is "how widely managers may vary in the way they spend their time. The differences are sometimes so great that they show how misleading it can be to talk about *the manager's* job or about how the average manager spends his time". For example, in the 1967 Stewart study, the time spent on all paper work was on average 36% which included only 2% on reading externally produced information. However, one accountant spent up to 84% of his time on paperwork and, as stated in table eight, seven managers spent between 10% and 15% of their time on external reading.

Glover maintains that as most managers are specialists of one kind or another, and the function of managing so diverse; the title, 'manager', appears almost meaningless.

Table 8 Empirical studies of managerial work activities

Researcher	Year reported	Method used	Managers studied	No. of work days studied	Study focus	Data on use of published information
Aguilar	1967	Interview	200 top managers	not applicable based on interview response	largely strategic environmental data	19% of all responses cited publications as an important external source and this broke down into 11% newspapers 9% journals (errors due rounding)
Austin	1975	Diary	36 local government officers	200	how officers spend their time	Time spent on articles/journals/books 3% with only four respondents recording more than 10%
Brewer and Tomlinson	1964	Diary	6 senior managers	105	how managers spend their time	Made distinction between general external reading (average 4%) and internal reports memos (average 9%)
Burns	1957	Diary	76 senior and middle managers	1520	how managers spend their time	Proportion of time spent reading 2-4% but one executive spent as much as 16% and three others spent 6%, 10% and 13% respectively
Carlson	1951	Diary	9 managing directors	216	how managers spend their time	None
Copeman	1963	Diary	58 senior and middle managers	290	how managers spend their time	5% of time spent on reading but type of reading not specified
Horne and Lupton	1965	Diary	66 middle managers	330	how managers spend their time	10% of time spent on reading but again type of reading not specified

Keegan	1968	Questionnaire	50 chief executives	not applicable data based on responses	study of sources of key information concerning the environment	Time spent on face to face contact 67% documents 27% (but these not categorised) and 6% on physical inspection
Kelly	1969	Activity sampling	4 section managers	2800 random observations	how managers spend their time	No data on documentation impact but the conclusion is that task is the principal determinant that structures the behaviour of the managers studied
Mintzberg	1967-8	Structured observation	5 chief executives	202 *hours*	how managers spend their time	Out of 659 pieces of information received 16% were periodical parts and 1% were books. In terms of output there were only 206 reactions to the 659 inputs. Out of the total output only 9% was as a result of published information ie books periodicals clippings. More specifically on periodicals coming in, action was taken on only 4 of the 102 received in the period
Stewart	1967	Diary	160 senior and middle managers	3200	how managers spend their time with special emphasis on differences	Most managers spend very little time reading, the average being 2%. Seven managers spent from 10-15% of time on external reading although one of these spent part of that time on reading tenders

Table 8 (contd.)

Researcher	Year reported	Method used	Managers studied	No. of work days studied	Study focus	Data on use of published information
Stewart	1976	(a) interview	mainly senior and middle	not applicable	data used to produce a classification of managerial jobs	No specific data but author (1977) maintains that the project[1] type manager is the one most likely to spend a relatively high proportion reading
		(b) interview and diary	mainly senior and middle	240	time analysis with the objective as above	
Thomason	1966-7	Diary	Various configurations of managers	not reported	how managers spend their time	Wide variations in time spent on written communication ranging from 51% to 12% with an average of 25%. No separate figures available for reading

[1] This type of work is characterised by long term tasks of a one-off nature and a greater need for sustained attention than the other types identified by the author.

Mintzberg et al maintain that it is functional specialisation that is the most single important ingredient affecting an individual manager's approach to his work. It is also a conclusion reached by Afanasev based on a study of 210 managers in which she concluded that the information needs of management workers are defined largely by their functional responsibilities and the nature of their management tasks; and by Kelly in a study of section managers at Glacier Metal. However Rosemary Stewart (1976 and 1977) produced a classification based on work patterns rather than specialisms and grouped managers into four distinct catagories. It was type three, the 'project manager', who she maintained was likely to read more. This work pattern is characterised by (1) much non-recurrent work, (2) the need for sustained attention, (3) much work that originates with the individual who has to be self generating, (4) much work that has a time horizon of more than one year.

The general conclusion presented in table eight that managers spend little time on reading published information clearly has to be modified, in that it disguises some significant variations in management jobs. Another difficulty about the evidence is that it was frequently not possible to ascertain the proportion of reading time spent on internal memos, letters, etc and that spent on publications. It is worth emphasising that as Thomason points out that it is assumed that managerial activities and communications form a pattern and are not accidentally or randomly distributed through time.

The overall conclusion is therefore, that managers generally read very little but there are very significant differences between managers and hopefully the fieldwork will shed more light on this. In addition the information services of the Institute only set out to meet a portion of a manager's information requirements in contrast with the Access service which did attempt to provide all the information relevant to the work of the design staff. Clearly the penetrative measures used in the BIM fieldwork will have to be modified to take these differences into account as well as the fact that the BIM membership will not necessarily use the Management Information Centre on a first resort basis, again in contrast with the Access user.

The organization
The British Institute of Management was founded in 1947 following the publication of the report of the Baillieu Committee who perceived the Institute's key aim "as raising the standards of management practice in the wider or more general sense as distinct from specialist management function of administration in the purely industrial field". More recently the Institute (1973) has restated its aims to be "furthering the improvement of individual and collective standards of management throughout the economy and to this end assisting in the training and development of the best managerial talents and in the more effective use and deployment of proven and successful techniques of management as they emerge from the public and private sectors".

Thus the role of the Institute is primarily an educational one, although recently the Institute has also placed some emphasis on providing a 'third voice' to articulate the management viewpoint in public life in possible contrast with those of the Confederation of British Industry and the Trade Unions Congress. Management was not defined in the restated aims but clearly the services offered by the Institute would be expected to contribute to these aims and thus implicitly define management in the context of the Institute.

These services include specialist advisory and information units concerned with physical distribution, management education, small business, management consultancy, executive remuneration, career counselling, industrial relations, management development, employee participation and financial management. The Institute distributes copies of *Management today* (published outside the Institute) and *Management reviews and digest* (published internally).

The Management Information Centre
The Centre has a staff of nineteen and has a total budget of £109,500 per annum (1978 figures) of which approximately £15,000 is spent on acquisitions. As has already been indicated the service primarily focuses on providing information and the loan of publications on management, management techniques and the major management functions of personnel, production, marketing and finance.

In addition to a large library, the Centre maintains a large collection of cases studies and unpublished company documentation including recruitment brochures, job specifications, appraisal forms, and pension booklets. The Centre produces about 170 bibliographies per annum; maintains a library catalogue; an optical coincidence retrieval system; and a number of specialist files of information.

Study outline
As with the GLC study, the BIM field work focuses on the interaction between the service and the customers at whom the service is aimed. The study however, in contrast with the GLC investigation, covers all the services offered by the Centre and therefore included all categories of use. The interview programme with users however, was restricted to those users who posed specific queries to the Centre as opposed to those using the lending and in-house reference facilities.

The study's main aim as with the GLC investigation was to establish how well the information distributed by the Centre was getting through to its members and what impact this information had on those managers receiving it. The study consisted of recording all[1] interactions with the service over a four week period and this data was then used to calculate penetration.

Impact data was collected by interview and questionnaire from *both* users and non users in an effort to compare the impact that specific items of published information made on the two groups. The impact data for non users was derived from the question "Can you recall the last occasion that you sought published information in connection with your work and managerial activities?" This was similar to an approach used by both Rosenbloom and Wolek and Vickery et al (1969).

Penetration data
Attempting to apply the concept of penetration in the context of BIM poses a number of difficulties, the most fundamental of which is that the Institute does not possess

---

[1] 649 interactions but many of the returns were incomplete so actual figures are given in each table. Seasonal variations as with the GLC study were therefore ignored.

extensive data on the characteristics of the audience that it is attempting to serve. The only data that is available is that produced by Melrose-Woodman (1978). This data was obtained from a 20% sample randomly drawn from the total *individual* membership list. Immediately therefore the data ignores the non individual member manager who is working in organisations that are collective subscribers (ie organisational members) who are also entitled to use the Management Information Centre. It is assumed therefore that the characteristics of individual member managers are the same as non members working in collective subscriber organisations.

Of the 10,000 individual members who were sent the Melrose-Woodman questionnaire, 4,525[†] members returned the questionnaire giving a response rate of 45%. The analysis based on these responses will be compared with the Management Information Centre usage patterns to ascertain whether or not there are significant differences between the 'Melrose Woodman' manager and the Management Information Centre User.

Table 9 Regional comparison between the characteristics of the BIM Manager and BIM Management Information Centre user

Region[1]	BIM Manager[2] %	Centre user[3] %
Scotland	6	3
Wales	3	2
Northern Ireland/Eire	1	1
North West England	10	7
North East England	13	6
Midlands	15	10
South West England	4	3
East Anglia	3	2
Southern England	33	23
Greater London	12	44
Totals	100	101[4]

[1] regional allocation criteria were identical
[2] based on 4,448 respondents
[3] based on 584 user responses
[4] error in this and subsequent tables due to rounding

[†] The total Institute individual membership was, at the time the survey was conducted, 50,000 which represents an overall response rate of just over 9%.

The significance of this data is that a large proportion of the users come from either the Greater London area or Southern England, whilst clearly the regional membership breakdown is more dispersed. It is possible however that the high proportion of London users is partly accounted for by the manager who works in London but resides outside; as no attempt in the user study was made to ensure that the regional allocation was based on a single consistent criterion of residence or employment. The Melrose Woodman data on the other hand was based almost exclusively on residence. Notwithstanding this there does still appear to be a regional imbalance in the penetration mix that the Centre is achieving. Perhaps this balance can be redressed by vigorously promoting the service except in the London and Southern areas and possibly by establishing some regional services especially in the heavily member populated regions of the North East, the North West and the Midlands.

The classification employed by the Institute in table ten is based on the Standard Industrial Classification and is riddled with cross classification eg should managers working for the National Coal Board be allocated to 'Mining' or 'Nationalized Undertakings'. The user study deliberately employed the same classification but because of these ambiguities, not too much reliance can be placed on either set of data. The comparatively high user figures listed under Financial/Professional Services and Education/Training may be accounted for by a disproportionate usage by academics and management consultants and this will be commented on further in the comparison of management functions. 69% of BIM managers worked in the private sector as compared with only 31% who worked in the public sector. Ignoring the deficiencies of the classification however, only 53% of the users worked in the private sector and 47% in the public, suggesting possibly yet another imbalance in the customer mix.

Comparison again was difficult because of the ambiguities of the classification but the most startling figure is the imbalance between the two personnel and training listings which include those working in academic institutions. There are four possible explanations for this difference: (1) personnel managers read more because this

Table 10 Comparison between the characteristics of the BIM managers employer and the Centres users employer

Employer Activity[1]	BIM manager[2] %	Centre user[3] %
Manufacturing	43	36
Mining & Construction	4	3
Transport/Communication	1	2
Distributive trades	6	4
Printing/Publishing	2	2
Financial Professional Services	8	16
Other services	6	11
Nationalized undertakings	11	4
Central government	2	3
Local Government/Water	4	2
Education/Training	11	16
Armed services	2	0
Health, Police, Fire & others	1	4
Total	101	98

[1] allocation criteria identical
[2] based on 4,296 respondents
[3] based on 533 respondents

Table 11 A comparison of managerial functions

Function	BIM manager[4] %	BIM user[5] %
General management	32	13
Production	6	3
Purchasing	2	category not included
Sales/Marketing	7	8
Distribution	1	category not included
Finance	6	5
Administration	9	8
Personnel/training	16	34
Management Services	9	14
Technical & Scientific	11	6
Other	category not included	8
Total	99	99

[4] 4,095 respondents
[5] 400 responses including a small number of multiple responses and excluding 118 library and information users. It was originally intended to question all user librarians to ascertain ultimate user but this did not prove possible.

is a characteristic of the type of person involved in personnel work; (2) personnel problems are the most difficult ones to solve and thus personnel managers use published information more frequently than their colleagues from other management functions; (3) more relevant published information is available on personnel topics compared with other functions; (4) it is a reflection of the history of the Institute's library which at one time offered its services to Institute of Personnel Management members. Whatever the explanation it represents another mismatch between the audience at which the service is aimed and those actually using the service.

Another difficulty in measuring penetration is that the Management Information Centre will frequently be used on a last resort basis and therefore one could not, as one did with the GLC data, assume that for information required by managers the Centre should always be used on a first resort basis. In addition there was no data comparable to the Goodey and Mathew daily requirement for product information which could have been used to crudely indicate the total need for published information in a management context. These difficulties were exacerbated by the large

Table 12 Surrogate use

Number of queries posed in four week period	Nature of use S = surrogate D = direct	Number of of enquirers	Total number of queries
Six queries	S	2	12
Five queries	S	2	10
Four queries	S	4	16
Three queries	S	5	15
Two queries	S	16	32
Two queries	D	13	26
One query	S	—	82
One query	D	—	444
Incomplete	—	—	16
	Total usage		653
	Total surrogate usage		183
	Total direct use		470

Data based on total record of all usage during a four week consecutive period amount of surrogate use particularly, but not exclusively, by librarians on behalf of managers as illustrated in table twelve.

The final penetration calculations were restricted to an analysis as to how well the Centre was reaching the people at whom the service was aimed. As table twelve indicates there were 444 direct users who used the service once plus 13 users who used the service twice. If one assumes that surrogate usage broke down in the same fashion, one produces visit frequency data of 172 using the service once and five using it twice during the four week period. One then establishes the following visit frequency data:

1 visit	444 + 172	=	616	single visits
2 visits	13 + 5	=	18	double visits

However only 25% of this usage was by individual members so that frequency data that was finally employed was 154 single visits and 5 double visits. Again this is based on a possibly invalid assumption that individual members used the Centre on the same frequency basis as all users. The 154 single visit and 5 double visit data was fed into the Brookes theorem as was the data presented for the GLC study. On the basis of this theorem the Centre would be expected to reach 2564 individual members or 5% of the total audience that it was attempting to reach. These calculations are somewhat dubious and reflect the difficulty of applying penetration to a library that is frequenty used indirectly and is almost always used on a last resort basis.

Also a much smaller proportion (17%) of multiple usage was identified in the BIM study and this 17% assumes that all surrogate use is on behalf of the same individual. This last assertion is of course clearly not true and originally it was the intention to determine who the actual user was on whose behalf the surrogate was enquiring. I have however been advised by B C Brookes that the theorem still applies to data obtained from a last resort (or at least not an inevitably first resort library of the GLC inhouse type) library which the BIM exemplifies.

The use and impact of published information
The study employed both questionnaire and interview and the responses are as given in table thirteen.

Table 13 Survey responses

Member category	Response form	Total sample	Total responses	Response rate
Non users	Q	800	289	36%
Information service users	I	41	28	68%
Other users	Q	248	112	45%
Total		1089	429[1]	39%

Q = questionnaire
I = interview

[1] excludes a small number of additional late returns.

1 *Non users* 800 questionnaires were sent out to a computerized randomly selected sample of non users. Non users were defined as individual member managers who were not recorded as using the service during the four week interaction study.

2 *Informaton service users* It had already been agreed that the interview programme was to be restricted to users of the information service rather than to book lending and other facilities. 166 such requests were recorded in the four week period and a one in four systematic† sample was taken. No direct refusals to participate were encountered and the failures broke down as follows: seven were never arranged because a date could not be agreed by the deadline; three managers had been posted abroad; three had given false addresses and one had retired. The interviews employed the questionnaire as a basis for the interview and and as in the GLC study the interviewees were actually shown the items that they had borrowed and returned.

3 *Other users* A systematic one in two sample was taken taken of the remaining users of the other Centre facilities.

A reminder was sent to all participants resulting in 87 additional responses (included in table thirteen) confirming the value of persistence. The questionnaire was pilot tested by approximately 28 managers.

The classification of external information sought, presented in table fourteen, was based on answers to the

---

† Moser and Kalton define systematic sampling as where the selection of one sample member is dependent on the selection of the previous one.

Table 14 Classification of external information sought

Information Category[1]	No.	Percent
Management Principles & Techniques	120	16
Education Training Courses	19	3
Compensation/Incentives	32	4
Other Personnel Topics	65	9
Technical Information	76	10
Product Equipment Data	38	5
Market Data	36	5
Statistical Data	31	4
Financial Taxation/Credit	53	7
Government Legislation	53	7
Other Legal Contractual Information	26	3
Information about Consultants	2	0
Surveys of Company Practice	25	3
Economic Data	20	3
Industry/Company Data	37	5
Current Affairs	7	1
Overseas Data	18	2
Bibliographical Information	13	2
Unclassified Responses[2]	41	5
Too varied to generalise	18	2
Other categories	30	4
	760	100

[1] These categories were based on an analysis of the open ended responses

[2] Responses such as information relevant to the problem, general background information etc.

question; "What kind of information are you generally seeking from this outside organization?"†

It is significant that only 16% of all responses cited management principles and techniques as an area for which they sought information from outside, although it was the most frequently recorded response. If one compares this 16% figure with the number of times non users, actual users and claimed users cite this area significant differences appear in the relative weights given to this category of information.

It appears therefore that actual users and claimed users

---

† The preceding question was 'When you wish to obtain information which is not available from within the work organization in connection with your work and management activities, to which outside organization do you most frequently resort?'

Table 15 Relative weight given to management principles & technique type information

Category	Total responses	Management responses	Percent
Non user	296	30	10
Actual user	213	50	23
Claimed users	182	32	18

have a much greater requirement for information on management principles and techniques than the non user. This could be a possible explanation of the poor penetrative performance of the Centre in that non users appear not to require this type of information as frequently as the user. Non users' key area of interest was technical information whilst financial/government legislation and management principles were roughly all equal second. In contrast the key area for users was management principles with technical information some way behind in second place.

If it is a valid assumption that non users are less interested in management principle type information it raises the question as to whether the Centre wishes to reach more non users by widening the scope of its provision. If however it deliberately restricts its remit to management principles and related areas then some method must be found to stimulate non user interest in these topics.

The next table analyses the answers to the question as to whether respondents could recall the last occasion that they they had used published information.

It was interesting here to discover that 85% of respondents could recall the last instance of having used published information suggesting that this is a more important managerial resource that other studies have indicated. This is also borne out by the data gathered in the study on time spent on managerial and work related reading which ranged from one hour per week to an unbelievable 60 hours per

Table 16 Recall of last use of published information

Recall	All respondents	Percent	Non users	Percent	Actual users	Percent	Claimed users	Percent
Yes	337	85	121	74	101	96	87	90
No	60	15	42	26	4	4	9	10
Total	397	100	163	100	105	100	96	100

week. Full details are given of this in the BIM publication (Blagden 1980).

Those that could recall their last use were asked what type of information they were seeking the results of which are given below.

Table 17 Published information analysis

Information Category	No.	Percent
Management principles	60	12
Education training courses	14	3
Compensation incentives	26	5
Other personnel topics	80	16
Technical information	34	7
Product equipment data	29	6
Market Data	18	4
Statistical data	7	1
Financial/taxation/credit/data	41	8
Government legislation	27	5
Other legal contractual information	13	3
Information about consultants	1	0
Surveys of company practice	13	3
Economic data	6	1
Industry/company data	35	7
Current affairs	0	0
Overseas data	22	4
Bibliographical information	13	3
Unclassified responses	43	9
Too varied to generalise	1	0
Other categories	21	4
Total	504	101

There is a similarity between the data presented here and table fourteen which analyses external information seeking patterns. The only difference is the much greater use of published information on personnel topics. User and non user differences are again much in evidence. Non users most searched for published information was 'Other personnel topics' followed by 'Technical information' whilst in contrast actual users still maintained a preference for 'Management principles' information with 'Other personnel topics' coming second. This table supports the assertion made earlier that there are two options open to the Centre in order to reach the non user by either stimulating a greater interest in management principles or changing the range of information offered by the Centre.

Table 18 Classification of BIM information sought

Information category	No.	Percent
Management principles	72	24
Education/training information	8	3
Compensation incentives	21	7
Other Personnel topics	49	16
Technical information	7	2
Product equipment data	6	2
Market data	10	3
Statistical data	2	1
Financial/taxation/credit	19	6
Government legislation	5	2
Other legal contractual information	6	2
Information about consultants	1	0
Surveys of company practice	8	3
Economic data	2	1
Industry/company data	5	2
Current affairs	0	0
Overseas data	8	3
Bibliographical information	22	7
Unclassified responses	37	12
Too varied to generalise	0	0
Other categories	13	4
Total	301	100

As would be expected Table 18 shows that in a management library about one in four requests appear to be in the management principle area, with 'Other personnel topics' also showing strongly as it has on all three tables. Other personnel topics includes industrial relations, recruitment and interviewing. If the classification had grouped together 'Education' and 'Training' with 'Compensation' and 'Incentives' and 'Other personnel topics' then information on personnel topics would appear to be the dominant requirement for the BIM user.

Table nineteen establishes the BIM benefit mix, and this can be compared with both table twenty, the benefit mix that managers generally achieve in their use of published information, and table twenty one, which details the benefit mix that the 28 managers who were interviewed achieved. As the bulk of these responses were obtained from questionnaires one could not probe the nature of the benefits gained by the respondents in using published information. I took the view here that one had to employ a somewhat simple minded scale highly relevant, relevant etc; although the questionnaire did make it clear that it was relevance to the problem, rather than topic relevance.

If one compares table nineteen with table twenty it appears that managers using the BIM Management Information Centre are marginally less successful than managers general use of published information. However table nineteen includes the interview data where it was possible to probe and obtain more realistic assessments of the benefits conferred by using published information. Even so if the BIM 'highly relevant' and 'relevant, but did not entirely answer the question' responses are added together it still gives an 80% success rate, compared with the 92% in the general table.

Where respondents indicated more than one form these are separately identified in tables nineteen and twenty. However the respondents usually only gave a *single* rating so in the combined all forms column this has been counted as a single rating, rather than a multiple rating response. Hence individual form totals when added together generally exceed the combined all forms totals.

However in some cases the form of publication was not given and in a minority of cases (including of course all the interview responses which are incorporated in table twenty) multiple *rating* responses were given. Clearly therefore the interview ratings given are more reliable than tables nineteen and twenty as they are based on ratings of each individual publication supplied. What does appear undeniable however is that tables nineteen and twenty demonstrate that library usage does generally appear successful even if within that successful usage marginally relevant or irrelevant publications are supplied.

If one compares tables nineteen and twenty with the interview data the picture is less encouraging in that only 55% of the documents supplied by the Centre appeared to be of much help. If however one reanalyses the data on the basis of how many of the 28 interviewees were provided with relevant or highly relevant publications then 21 out of the 28 interviewees fall into this category, ie 75%. This is of course explained by the fact that the majority of questionnaire respondents provided a single benefit response to which reference was made earlier. These responses may well therefore have ignored the less favourable items that

Table 19 Benefits of searches — last use of BIM

Manager Rating	All forms Total	All forms Percent	Books Total	Books Percent	Newspapers Total	Newspapers Percent	Journals Total	Journals Percent	Other publications Total	Other publications Percent
Highly relevant	121	48	77	60	6	55	28	52	34	51
Relevant	81	32	34	27	4	36	22	41	24	36
Marginally relevant	42	17	17	13	1	9	4	7	6	9
Irrelevant	10	4	0	0	0	0	0	0	2	3
Total	254	101	128	100	11	100	54	100	66	99

Table 20 Benefits of searches — last use of published information

Manager Rating	All forms Total	All forms Percent	Books Total	Books Percent	Newspapers Total	Newspapers Percent	Journals Total	Journals Percent	Other publications Total	Other publications Percent
Highly relevant	219	64	119	64	7	44	50	53	91	63
Relevant	98	28	49	26	7	44	36	38	48	33
Marginally relevant	21	6	17	9	2	12	8	9	5	3
Irrelevant	3	1	1	1	0	0	0	0	0	0
Total	341	99	186	100	16	100	94	100	144	99

Table 21 Benefits of searches last use of BIM – interviewee ratings

Manager rating	All forms Total	All forms Percent	Books Totals only	Newspapers Totals only	Periodicals Totals only	Other publications Totals only
Highly relevant	17	26	11	1	4	1
Relevant	19	29		nil	8	2
Marginally relevant	26	40	18	nil	8	nil
Irrelevant	3	5	3	nil	nil	nil
Total[1]	65	100	41	1	20	3

[1] Total number of publications shown to the 28 interviewees

they retrieved because, as long as some useful publications were supplied, the user would register overall satisfaction. One issue therefore to be clarified in any future studies of this kind, especially in university and special libraries, is does one assess performance on the basis of individual documents distributed by the library or on the basis of whether a particular library usage did contribute to the task in hand. Neither approaches are mutually exclusive and depend to a large extent on how usage is defined, but the weakness here is that it is not clear as to the basis on which respondents are replying.

It certainly confirms that the interview is the most effective method here, as the questionnaires would have to be very elaborate indeed to distinguish these two assessment approaches. A point made by a number of interviewees was that by emphasizing problem solution the study may well have de-emphasized other benefits obtained from library usage in terms of problem definition and general thought clarification. Another difficulty that emerged in the interviews was that I discovered that asking questions about reading was more threatening than I had imagined. There was on one hand the manager who was clearly reluctant to admit that he read at all, because, my impression was, that if he admitted he read he was also admitting to being less dynamic/overworked etc than his colleagues. My evidence for this view was that under his desk he had a brief case literally bulging with management journals. Conversely there was the personnel officer who read very little but felt very guilty about it and perhaps again this attitude influenced her responses.

This more extensive study appears to confirm the tentative conclusion reached in the GLC fieldwork that libraries are not getting many 'messages' through to their customers, but those that do get through do generally appear to make a favourable impact.

In terms of the BIM's apparently poor penetrative performance the investigation was limited by the same problem, as with the GLC, as to what the right degree of penetration should be. However a service that is unlikely to reach more than 5% of its members and where also there does appear to be significant mismatches in terms of the general characteristics of the user and non user, strongly suggests that reacting to demand is not enough. Also penetration was limited to one class of membership and clearly what is required is more information on the characteristics of non individual member managers working in collective subscriber organizations. If this is not possible then the kind of penetration calculations that have been presented here, could be reworked in terms of how well the Centre is reaching collective subscriber organizations (as opposed to individual based penetrative calculations).

Again in the GLC study reference was made to the closed nature of the system in that users were very much conditioned by what was available from the service. Similarly the Centre provides information on management principles and techniques which appears to be of significantly less interest to the non user. The study has made explicit, therefore, the dilemma facing the Institute as to whether it provides all the significant published information that managers require or deliberately restricts its remit, as it does now. Tables fourteen, seventeen and eighteen provide evidence which can be used to review the policies of what information the Centre should provide in the future.

The study has also established a tentative dialogue with its customers and this should be maintained so that the service, continually and systematically gathers customer feedback. How this should be achieved is perhaps a problem but some user panel arrangement based on the extensive BIM branch structure might provide the answer here.

If one believes that penetration should be improved, then inevitably this will result in a greater use being made of the Centre's facilities. If resources are not increased to meet this increased demand, then the quality of the service will drop and demand will soon fall back to, or below, its original level. The impact data has shown that published information disseminated by the Centre, appears to yield considerable benefits to those managers who use these facilities. Thus the Centre supports one of the key aims of the Institute of "furthering the improvement of individual and collective standards of management throughout the economy". The impact data collected, however, needs considerable refinement and would have been more reliable if it had all been collected by interview rather than postal questionnaires.

The Centre and probably the Institute as a whole needs to establish some method of ensuring that resources match demand so that costs of information supply are recovered. Otherwise the Centre will continue to be a purely reactive institution without necessarily managing the demands placed upon it so that it maximises the benefit mix that it wishes to achieve.

EIGHT

PERFORMANCE ASSESSMENT – WHERE DO WE GO FROM HERE?

Penetration
In both the GLC and BIM studies, penetration appears to be a viable concept for evaluating the performance of a library, in that it provides a systematic way of assessing how well library messages are getting through to the audience at which they are aimed. Dividing the audience into homogeneous market segments and simply comparing numbers in each segment with the degree of penetration by the library can be a useful and relatively painless exercise to implement. Penetrative measures can be widened to include many additional user characteristics other than work task (which would appear to be a key factor) such as region, place of work, work stage, professional discipline and type of employer.

A major difficulty, however, has been to establish what the library share of the market ought to be in order to achieve optimum results. In the GLC, the Goodey & Mathew data was employed to indicate crudely the size of the information need market that the library was trying to penetrate. More data of this sort needs to be established for differing customer groups and hopefully the data can be based on the use of reliable methodology such as activity sampling. In addition any data collected must examine the organizational factors that affect the use of a library, for example, in the GLC what the likely effect would be of personal collections of trade literature on the use of the Access service. In the more difficult situation in the BIM, studies of penetration must include some attempt to quantify the fact that frequently the Management

Information Centre would be used on a last rather than first resort basis.

Impact
Whether impact ie attempting to determine both the degree of cognitive enrichment resulting in the receipt of a library message and any outcomes, is as useful an evaluative technique appears to be much more of an open question for the following reasons:

1 There is the difficulty of assessing the long term effect of reading and the problem of distinguishing benefit to the individual from benefit to the organization funding the library or benefits to society as a whole.

2 Once impact data is collected are there any steps that the library manager can take to improve his mix of benefit/disbenefit mix? Clearly a weakness of the fieldwork is that the impact data collected was not really specific enough to answer that question. This was partly due to utilizing the questionnaire as the main method of gathering such data; as it is clear that a face to face dialogue with the user provides the opportunity to probe which is vital to the collection of useful data. In addition face to face contact enables the user to be confronted with publications that he has borrowed which was certainly very successful, in obtaining what appeared to be useful fact based responses. It is worth emphasizing here, that even if the concept of impact does not appear to be worth pursuing, certainly the simple device of showing users publications that they have borrowed, does appear a useful way of obtaining reliable user responses as perhaps a validation of more generalised responses in a user study.

3 In addition to the impact data not being specific enough to ascertain the benefit/disbenefit mix it also failed to tackle the question of corporate contribution. At this stage this would appear again to be a fault of the way the fieldwork was carried out involving mainly questionnaires rather than interview. In addition of course the BIM aimed its services at a large number of individual members where the evaluation of impact could quite legitimately be restricted to impact on that individual manager.

Corporate contribution ought to be more overtly included in any further impact studies and the idea of the

Allen super judge ought to be considered. Perhaps corporate contribution could then be assessed both by the individual library message recipient and those who were also exposed to the message within the organization, albeit indirectly.

4 No replicated studies have been conducted here, ie collecting two sets of impact data from the same library system to ascertain if the impact mix remains reasonably constant. It may be therefore that the library system is not a critical factor at all and the impact of the library message is dependent on factors largely outside the librarian's control. Certainly as indicated in tables one and two, both high performing and low performing research and development personnel had an almost identical work pattern including time spent on published information. This would appear to suggest that the critical variable here is the ability of the engineers themselves, rather than their use of the various information transfer channels.

5 No comparative data was collected on the impact of the three main ways that information is transferred (oral, letter, publication) and therefore no progress was made on a key theme of this book as to whether the channels can be managed for effective knowledge utilization. However it was interesting to note in the BIM study that in external information seeking, publication appeared to be the dominant channel amongst managers; a group who in the past have been thought to rely more heavily on other channels. If one allies this to the impact data that was collected in the BIM study on both generalised usage of published information and the specific Centre usage, considerable benefits appear to accrue to managers who use published information.

Now clearly in establishing impact, there were some deficiencies in the fieldwork but no evidence has emerged (as was expected) that a great deal of the use of published information is of little benefit to the user. Impact data can be used therefore not necessarily as a means of effectively managing the benefit/disbenefit mix, but simply as evidence which demonstrates the value and range of benefits that can be obtained by both the use of libraries and published information.

6 It may be therefore that the library's role should be to

maximise usage because generally usage appears to benefit the user. More work would have to be done on collecting more refined impact data than that cited in chapters six and seven, before this could be assumed to be true, even for the two libraries participating in the fieldwork. There is also obviously no evidence to suggest that even if this were true for these two special libraries, that it is necessarily true for other special libraries.

7 If the collection of reliable impact data does result in more aggressive library marketing policies it would raise not only resource problems, but also the question as to what effect these policies would have on other channels of communication. Library usage could be increased to such an extent, that the usage does become disbeneficial to both the user and the funding organization. The library manager must therefore still continue to take the wider view that he is concerned with maximising only beneficial usage rather than promoting all library usage.

After reviewing the various approaches that have been made to the problem of evaluating library performance it was concluded in chapter five that none of these approaches appeared to give any indication as to how effective libraries are in transferring knowledge. Yet libraries exist to enrich the minds of men and women, and if they fail to do this, then the initial investment in the library would not appear to be justified.

Orr of course has developed a method of evaluating document delivery without which no knowledge transfer can take place, but an efficient delivery system can only be regarded as an intermediate stage in the effective transfer of knowledge. Other attempts to put a money value on the information supplied by the library assume that the information distributed has benefited the individual or organisation, without providing any evidence to support the assertion. Allen has of course shown that messages emanating directly from published sources do not appear to have a very significant impact on corporate performance. Although this work was clearly a major piece of research on the effectiveness of the information transfer capability of various channels it did not shed much direct light on library performance.

The fieldwork described in chapters six and seven

attempted therefore to provide some complementary data on the performance of two libraries, utilising the concepts of penetration and impact. Despite the many difficulties that have been experienced both at the GLC and the BIM it is still believed that these two concepts provide a possible way forward for those concerned with evaluating the performance of libaries. Even if these techniques in the long run do prove to be impractical, the author has no doubt that library performance measures must increasingly be based on the outputs and outcomes of the system rather than the resources that are put into a library. In short, library managers must ensure that their services become more customer oriented rather than book oriented and in so doing counteract the stable unchanging relationship that libraries have with their customers. A systematic dialogue therefore needs to be established that opens up this relationship so that a library's performance can be continually assessed in terms of how well it is meeting both user needs and corporate goals.

Just before completing this book I read a fine piece of devil's advocacy polemic by Don Revill who stated:

1 you cannot do research in librarianship;
2 and if you can:
   (i) it should not be called research; and,
   (ii) it cannot be generalised to any other library or situation;
3 but if it can no one does so because they cannot understand it;
4 and if they did they would not accept it;
5 and if they did they would be deluding themselves because it would not work.

This made me feel a little uneasy but I was reassured slightly when he stated that he would have no quarrel with those who conducted research, providing the word research was dropped and the word investigation or enquiry substituted. Certainly the work described in the second half of this book is much more of an enquiry or investigation rather than research although hopefully none the worse for this.

Many books end with a plea for more research (sic) and I am afraid this one is going to be no exception. What the profession requires is a sustained attack on the problem of developing a methodology by which the performance of a library can be more effectively assessed. We need, in my view, to make this a key priority over the next decade and hopefully the Cranfield Social Policy Unit's unique practioner-based research programme will attract sufficient MSc/PhD candidates from librarianship to make some contribution here. We also need to establish a performance assessment information bank so that librarians have some external source that they can tap when faced with a need for justificatory data. It is hoped that this book will help here, but as librarians do not make as effective use of professional literature as they should, there is a continuing requirement for an organization to act as an interface between performance assessment research investigations and the practitioner.

Above all we want to move from a defensive position into the attack because none of the work that I have reported appears remotely to suggest that libaries are not very good for you. We need however constantly to demonstrate this in all types of library and therefore in my view a major part of the professions's resources needs to be channelled in this direction. If we do not do so we only have ourselves to blame, if resources allocated to libraries continue to diminish.

BIBLIOGRAPHY

ADELSON, R M and Norman, J M Operations research and decision making *Operational research quarterly* 20 (4) 1969, 399-413

AFANASEV, E V *Information support for management, scientific and technical information processing* 1976 (3) 1-6

AGUILAR, F J *Scanning the business environment* Macmillan 1967

ALLEN, T J Communication networks in R & D laboratories *R & D Management* October 1970 1 (1) 14-21

ALLEN, T J *Managing the flow of technology* MIT 1977

ANDRUS, R R Approaches to information evaluation *MSU Business topics* 1971 Summer 40-45

ARMSTRONG, C M Measurement and evaluation of the public library In *Research methods in librarianship: measurement and evaluation* ed H Goldhor, University of Illinois 1968

ATKIN, P Bibliography of use surveys of public and academic libraries 1950—Nov 1970 *Library and information bulletin* 14 1971 1-82

AUSTIN, B M *Effective use of time* Leicester Polytechnic 1975

BAILLIEU, Sir Clive (Chairman) *A central institute of management* Board of Trade, HMSO 1946

BARR, A et al *Wisconsin studies of the measure and prediction of teacher effectiveness* Dembar Publications 1961

BISHOP, D and Alsop, K *A study of coding and data co-ordination for the construction industry* HMSO 1969

BLAGDEN, J Information services to management consultants *Aslib proceedings*, November 1973 25 (11) 459

BLAGDEN, J Communication: a key library management problem *Aslib proceedings* 1975 27 (8) 319-326

BLAGDEN, J Special Libraries *Library Association record* 77 (6) June 1975, 129-133

BLAGDEN, J *Do managers read?* Cranfield Institute of Technology Press and British Institute of Management 1980.

BLAGDEN, J *Special libraries and corporate performance: the elusive connection* MA Thesis University College 1978

BOMMER, Michael Operational research in libraries: a critical assessment *Journal of the American Society for Information Science* May-June 1975 26 (3) 137-139

BONN, George Evaluation of the collection *Library trends* January 1974, 265-304

BOOKSTEIN, A and Swanson, D Introduction *Library quarterly* January 1972 42 (1) 1-5

BRAYBROOKE, D and Lindblom, C *Strategy of decision* Free Press Glencoe 1963

BRECH, E F L *The principles and practice of management* Longmans 1963

BREWER, E and Tomlinson, J W C The managers working day *Journal of industrial economics* 1964 12 191-197

BRITISH Institute of Management *BIM Future objectives — Council policy review* BIM 1973

BRITTAIN, J M *Information and its users: a review with special reference to the social sciences* Oriel 1970

BROOKES, B C A Sampling theorem for finite discrete distributions *Journal of documentation* March 1975 31 (1) 26-35

BROOKES, B C The estimation of populations engaged in intermittent activities in information contexts. *International forum on information and documentation* 1979 4 (2) 12-18

BROPHY, P et al *Reader in operations research in libraries* Microcard edition 1976

BUCKLAND, Michael K The management of libraries and information centres In Cuadra, CA *Annual review of information science and technology* American Society for Information Science 9 1974

BUCKLAND, M K *Book availability and the library user* Pergamon Press 1975

BUREAU of Applied Social Research *Review of studies in the flow of information among scientists* 1960

BURNETT, A D Economics and the university library *Universities quarterly* Autumn 1970 24 (4) 440-452

BURNS, Tom Management in action *Operation research quarterly* June 1957 8 2 45-60

BURR, R L Library goals and behaviour *College research libraries* 36 (1) Jan 1975 27-32

CALDER, Nigel *What they read and why: the use of technical literature in the electrical and electronic industries* HMSO 1959.

CAMPBELL, J P et al *Managerial behaviour performance and effectiveness* McGraw Hill 1970

CAREY, A The Hawthorne studies: A radical criticism *American sociological review* 32 (3) June 1967, 403-416

CARLSON, Sune *Executive behaviour* Stromberg 1951

CATHERWOOD, Fred *The Christian citizen* Hodder and Stoughton 1969

CAWKELL, A E Cost effectiveness and benefits of SDI systems *Information scientist* 1972 6 (4) 143-148

CHADDOCK, D H In R A Wall ed Seminar on mechanical engineering. Information provision and use Conference Proceedings Loughborough University 1974

CHILDERS, Thomas Community referral services: impact measures In *Information for the community* edited by M Kochen and J Donohue American Library Association

CLAPP, Verner W and Jordan, Roker T Quantitative criteria for the adequacy of academic library collections. *College and research libraries* Sept 1965 26 371-380

CLARK, P A *Action research and organizational change* Harper and Row 1972

COPEMAN, George et al *How the executive spends his time* Business Books 1963

COOPER, W S Letter *Journal of the American Society for Information Science* July/August 1976, 263-264

COOPER, W S On selecting a measure of retrieval effectiveness. *Journal of the American Society for Information Science* March/April 1973, 87-100 and Nov/Dec 1973 24 (6) 413-424

COOVER, R W User needs and their effect on information centre administration A review 1953-66 *Special libraries* 60 Sept 446-456

CUADRA, C A editor *Annual review of information science and technology* 1 — 10 1966-1975 American Society for Information Science

DAVIS, D L New approaches to studying library use *Drexel library quarterly* Jan 1971 4-12

DAVIS, R A How engineers use literature *Chemical engineering progress* 61 (3) 30-34 March 1965

DE BARRA F Building information a preliminary study in the needs of users of building information services. Unpublished typescript Building Department, University of Manchester Institute for Science and Technology, 1966.

DEHLINGER, H E A large scale architectural information system In *Information systems for designers* University of Southampton 1974

DEPT of the Environment *An Information system for the construction industry: final report of the working party on data co-ordination* HMSO 1971

DISCH, A The voice of the user *Agard conference* no 169 Agard 1976

DRAKE, B Data needs of the chartered quantity surveyor *Building* 17 March 1972 111-112

DRAKE, J Corporate planning and libraries: where are we now *Library management* 1 (1) 1979 1-72

DRIVER, M J and Mock, T J Human information processing, decision style theory and accounting information systems *Accounting review* July 1975, 490-508

DRUCKER, Peter Managing the Public Service Institution *Public interest* Fall 1973 33 43-60

ELINSON, Jack Methods of socio-medical research In M Freeman, Howard, Levin S and Reeder, L G *Handbook of medical sociology* Prentice Hall 1963

ELWEN, P D *Criteria for relevance decisions* MSc thesis, City University 1972

ENSOR, James Why British industry wastes £6 million a year on old information *Financial times* 29th December 1969, 23

EVANS, E et al Review of criteria used to measure effectiveness *Bulletin of the Medical Library Association* Jan 1972, 102-110

FABISOFF, S G and Ely, D P Information and information needs *Information reports and bibliographies* 1976 5 (5) 1-15

FARRAR, C H and Malthouse, R F W *Quantity Surveying product manufacture and merchanting* Current Paper 8/69 Building Research Station 1969

FAYOL, H *Administration industrielle et generale* Dunod 1916

FLANAGAN, J L The critical incident technique *Psychological bulletin* July 1954 51 (4) 327-358

FLOWERDEW, A D J and Whitehead, C M E Cost effectiveness and cost benefit analysis *OSTI report* 5206 London School of Economics and Political Science 1974

FORD, M G Research on user behaviour in university libraries *Journal of documentation* 29 85-106, 1973
FORD, M G *User studies* University of Sheffield 1977
FORES, M and Glover, I The real work of executives *Management today* November 1976, 104-108
FROST, Michael *Value for money: the techniques of cost benefit analysis* Gower Press 1972
GERSTBERGER, P G and Allen, T J Criteria used by research and development engineers in the selection of an information source *Journal of applied psychology* Aug 1968 52 (4) 272-279
GLOVER, I A *Managerial work: a review of the evidence* City University 1977
GODDARD, H C An economic analysis of library benefits *Library quarterly* July 1971, 244-255
GOODELL J S *Libraries and work sampling* Libraries Unlimited 1975
GOODEY, Jane and Matthew, Kate *Architects and information* Research Paper No 1 Institute of Advanced Architectural Studies University of York 1971
GRALEWSKA-VICKERY, A Communication and information needs of earth science engineers *Information processing and management* 12 (4) 1976, 251-282
GREENBERG, B G and Mattison, B F The whys and wherefores of program evaluation *Canadian journal of public health* 46 July 1955, 295-296
GUBA, Egon G and Stufflebeam, Daniel S *Evaluation: the process of stimulating aiding and abetting insightful action* Indiana University 1970
HALEY, R I Benefit segmentation: a decision oriented research tool *Journal of marketing* July 1968 32 30-35
HALL, A M *Methodology and results of some user studies on secondary information services* Eurim Conference 1973, Aslib 1974
HALL, R M S In R A Wall ed *Seminar on mechanical engineering information: provision and use.* Conference Proceedings. Loughborough University 1974
HALL, R W *An investigation into the information habits of scientists and engineers in industry* Indiana University 1969
HALL, R W Technical information habits of engineers *Chemical engineering progress* March 1973 69 (3) 67-71
HAMBURG, M et al *Library planning and decision making systems* MIT Press 1974
HAMILTON, D *Curriculum evaluation* Open Books 1976
HANEY, Roger, Harris, M H and Tipton, L The impact of reading on human behaviour In *Advances in librarianship* edited by M J Voigt and M H Harris Academic Press 6 1976
HANNAH, M *Basis of relevance decisions of information specialists* MSc thesis City University 1971
HANSON, C W Review of research and experimentation particularly in mechanical engineering *OSTI report* no 5202 Feb 1974
HARRISON, A J and Quarmby, D J M In Layard, R *Cost benefit analysis selected readings* Penguin 1974

HATT, F *The reading process: a framework for analysis and description* C Bingley 1976

HAVELOCK, R G *Bibliography on knowledge utilization and dissemination* Institute for Social Research University of Michigan 1972

HAVELOCK, R G et al *Planning for innovation through dissemination and utilization of knowledge* University of Michigan 1969

HAWGOOD, J and Morley, R Project for evaluating the benefits from University libraries Durham University 1969 *OSTI report* 5056

HAWGOOD, J and Morris, W E M Benefit assessment for system change in libraries and information services *Research and development report* University of Durham 1976

HILL, R W Some reflections on consumer panels *British journal of marketing* Summer 1969, 63-75

HILLS, J A *A review of the literature on primary communication in science and technology* Aslib 1972

HINDLE, A *Private communication* Nov 1976

HOLMES, P L *The role of information in science and technology* Report number 5180 Office for scientific and technical information 1974

HORNE, J H and Lupton, T The work activities of middle managers: an exploratory study *Journal of management studies* Feb 1965 2 (1) 14-23

HUNTER, Neil Library management *Management decision bibliography* MCB (Management Decision) Ltd 1974

INSTITUTE for Operational Research *The scope for operational research in the library and information services field: a report to OSTI* 10R 1972

JOHNSTON, J A survey of construction industry libraries *Aslib proceedings* Oct 1975 27 (10) 401-413

JUDGE, P J Cost effectiveness of information service criterion strategy or myth *(Australian special library news* June 1975 8 (2) 41-6

KEEGAN, W J *Information incentive* August 1968 11 11-13

KELLY, Joe *Organization behaviour* Holmwood 1969

KING, Donald W and Bryant Edward C *The evaluation of information services and products* Information Resources Press 1971

KING, D W and Palmour, V E User behaviour in *Changing patterns in information retrieval* American Society for Information Science 1973

KINGSTON upon Hull City Libraries *What why and how: MBO the library service* Kingston upon Hull 1971

KISH, L *Survey sampling* Wiley 1965

KNIGHT, Roy The measurement of reference use In *Output measurement* Public Libraries Research Group 1974

KRAMER, J How to survive in industry — cost justifying library services *Special Libraries* Nov 1971 62 (11) 487-489

KRANSBERG, M Formal versus informal communication among researchers In *Current research on scientific and technical information transfer* Jeffrey Norton Publishers 1977

KREVITT, B I and Griffith, B C Evaluation of information systems: a bibliography 1967-72 *Information* Part 2, 2 (6) 1973 1-34

KUEHL, Philip G Marketing viewpoints for user needs In *Economics of information dissemination: a symposium* edited by Robert S Taylor Syracuse University 1973

LADENDORF, Janice Information service evaluation: the gap between the ideal and the possible *Special libraries* July 1973 64 (7) 273-279

LANCASTER, F W The cost effectiveness analysis of information retrieval and dissemination systems *Journal of American Society for information science* 22 12-27, 1971

LANCASTER, F W *The measurement and evaluation of library services* Information Resources Press 1977

LANTZ, Brian E *Manual versus computerised reference retrieval in an academic library* MA thesis University College 1977

LAYARD, Richard *Cost benefit analysis: selected readings* Penguin Books 1974

LEAVITT, Theodore Marketing myopia *Harvard business review* July/August 1960, 45-56

LINDLEY, D V *Making decisions* Wiley Interscience 1971

LINE, Maurice The ability of a university library to provide books wanted by researchers *Journal of librarianship* January 1973 5 (1) 37-51

LINE, Maurice Draft definitions *Aslib proceedings* 1974 26 (2) 87

LINE, Maurice *Library surveys: an introduction to their use, planning and presentation* Bingley 1967

LUBANS, J On non use of an academic library *New York Library Association* 70 47-70 ND

LUFKIN, S M and Miller, E H The reading habits of engineers a preliminary survey *IEEE transactions on education* 1966, 9 (4) 1979-182

MAGSON, M S Techniques for the measurement of cost benefit analysis in information centres *Aslib proceedings* May 1973 25 (5) 164-185

MANN, Peter *Methods of sociological enquiry* Blackwell 1968

MARKUS, T A Cost-benefit analysis in building design: problems and solutions *Journal of architectural research* December 1976 5 (3) 22-33

MARSCHAK, J and Radner, R *Economic theory of teams* Yale University Press 1972

MARTYN, J and Vickery, B C The complexity of the modelling of information systems. *Journal of documentation* September 1970 26 (3) 204-220

MASON, D Programmed budgeting and cost effectiveness *Aslib proceedings* 1973 25 (3) 100-110

MASTERSON, W A Work study in a polytechnic library *Aslib proceedings* September 1976 28 (9) 288-304

McALPINE, A et al The flow and use of scientific information in University research Manchester Business School 1972 *(OSTI report 5138)*

McCAFFERTY, M Library information science bibliographies, guides, reviews, surveys *Aslib bibliography* No 3 Aslib 1976

McCLELLAN, A W Reading the other side of the equation *Journal of librarianship* Jan 1977 9 (1) 38-48

McDONOUGH, A M *Information economics and management systems* McGraw Hill 1963

McLUHAN, M *Understanding media* Routledge Kegan and Paul 1964

MEIER, R L Efficiency criteria for the operation of large libraries *Library quarterly* 31 1961, 215-234

MELROSE-WOODMAN, J E *Profile of the British manager* BIM 1978

MELROSE-WOODMAN, J E Profit centre accounting: the absorption of central overhead costs. *Management survey report No 21* British Institute of Management 1974

MENZEL, H Can science information needs be ascertained empirically In Thayer, L *Communication concepts and perspectives* Spartan Books 1967

MINISTRY of Public Building and Works *Data coordination in the civil engineering industry* R & D Paper Ministry of Public Building & Works 1970

MINTZBERG, H *The nature of managerial work* Harper and Row 1973

MOORE, N *A study of the development and the current state of public library research in Great Britain* British Library R & D report No 5419, 1978

MORIARTY, John H Measurement and evaluation in college and university library studies: library research at Purdue University. In *Research methods in librarianship measurement and evaluation by Herbert Goldor University of Illinois Graduate School of Library Science* 1968, 25-32

MOSER, C A and Kalton, G *Survey methods in social investigation* Heinemann 1971

MUNDAY, M Education for information management in the construction industry *Construction industry information group review* (3) Spring 1979, 11-22

MURDOCH J W and Liston, D M *A general model of information transfer* American Documentation October 1967 18 (4) 197-208

NEWTON, T *Cost benefit analysis in administration.* Allen & Unwin 1972

NOBLE, Pamela and Layzell-Ward, Patricia Performance measures and criteria for libraries: a survey and bibliography *PLRG occasional paper* No 3 Public Libraries Research Group 1976

NORDSTROM, K Designers information problems In *Information systems for designers* University of Southampton 1974

NORTH American Aviation Inc *Final report DOD users study phase 2 flow of scientific and technical information within the defense industry* Defense Documentation Center 1966

OLDMAN, Christine *A longitudinal study of the costs and benefits of academic library services* Unpublished draft 1976

OLDMAN, Christine M *The value of academic libraries: a methodological investigation* PhD Thesis Cranfield Institute of Technology 1978

OLSEN, H A The economics of information: bibliography and comments on the literature *Information* Part 2 March/April 1972 1 (2) 1-48

ORR, R H et al Development of methodologic tools for planning and managing library services I Project goals and approaches *Bulletin of the Medical Library Association* July 1968 56 (3) 235-240

ORR, R H et al Development of methodologic tools for planning and managing library services II Measuring a library's capability for providing documents *Bulletin of the Medical Library Association* July 1968 56 (3) 241-267

ORR, R H et al Development of methologic tools for Planning III Standardised inventories of library services *Bulletin of the Medical Library Association* October 1968 56 (4) 380-403

ORR, R H Development of methodological tools for planning and managing library services: bibliography of studies selected for methods data useful to biomedical libraries. *Bulletin of the Medical Libraries Association* 58 July 1970 350-377

ORR, R H Measuring the goodness of library services, a general framework for considering quantitative measure *Journal of documentation* 29 315-322, 1973

ORR, R H The scientist as an information processor In *Communication among scientists and engineers* edited by N Pollock Heath 1970

POLITZ Media Studies *A study of outside transit poster exposure* Alfred Politz 1959

PROPERTY Services Agency *Progress report No 2 on Data Coordination* PSA 1976

RAPPAPORT, A Sensitivity analysis in decision making In *Management decision making* edited by L A Welsch and R M Cyert Penguin Books 1970

REES, A M and Schulz D G *A field experimental approach to the study of relevance assessments in relation to document searching* Case Western Reserve University 1967

REVILL, Don You can't do research in librarianship *Library management news* (11) February 1980 10-25

REYNOLDS, Rose A selective bibliography on measurement in library and information services *Aslib* 1970

RICHARDSON, S A, Dohrenwend, B S and Klein, D *Interviewing its form and functions* Basic Books 1965

RITCHIE, E and Hindle, A *Communication networks in R & D: a contribution to the methodology and some results in a particular laboratory* University of Lancaster 1976

ROBERTS, M Use of periodicals in architecture *CIIG bulletin* Jan 71 7-12

ROBERTSON, A Behaviour patterns of scientists and engineers in information seeking for problem solving *Aslib proceedings* 1974 26 (10) 384-390

RODWELL, J *A review of the recent literature on the assessment of library effectiveness* University of New South Wales, School of Librarianship 1975

ROETHLISBERGER, F J and Dickson, W J *Management and the worker* Harvard University Press 1937

ROSENBERG, K C Evaluation of an industrial library: a simple minded technique *Special libraries* Dec 1969 60 (10) 635-638

ROSENBERG, Victor Studies in the man-system interface in libraries. Report No 2: The application of psychometric techniques to determine the attitudes of individuals towards information seeking. Lehigh University 1966

ROSENBLOOM, R S and Wolek, F W *Technology and information transfer* Harvard University 1970

SARACEVIC, T Relevance: a review of the literature and a framework for thinking on the notion in information science In *Advances in librarianship* edited by M J Voigt and M H Harris Academic Press 1976

SAMUELSON, K Systems design concepts for automated international information networks *ASIS proceedings* 5 431-435

SCHRENK, L P Aiding the decision maker a decision process model *Ergonomics* 12 (4) July 1969, 543-557

SHORT, E C A *A review of studies of the general problem of knowledge production and utilization* 1970, ED 055 022

SILVEY, Robert In Worcester, Robert M Where ratings don't rule *The observer* 11 April 1976, 19-22

SLATER, M and Fisher, P Use made of technical libraries *Aslib occasional pub* No 2 Aslib 1969

SMITH, H A *The use of panels for the collection of readership data* Thomson 1966

SNOW, Christine Architects wants and needs for information demonstrated through a university based information service *Aslib proceedings* March 1975 27 (3) 112-123

STECHER, G Library evaluation *(Australian academic and research libraries* March 1975 6 (1) 1-19

STEVENS, R F and Monument, L Structural engineering design *Current paper* 5/69 Building Research Station 1969

STEWART, R *Contrasts in management* McGraw Hill 1976

STEWART, R Letter to the author 1977

STEWART, R *Managers and their jobs* MacMillan 1967

SUCHMAN, Edward *Evaluative research: principles and practices in public service and social action programs* Russel Sage Foundation 1967

SUTTON, J R Information requirements of engineering designers *Agard conference proceedings* No 179 Agard 1976

SWANSON, R N Performance evaluation studies in information science *Journal of American society of information science* 26 140-156 1975

SWEENEY, G P The use of national resources to encourage the more effective use of information by industry *Aslib proceedings* Feb 1977 29 (2) 91-103

TAYLOR, Peter J *Library and information studies in the United Kingdom 1950-1974: an index to theses* Aslib 1976

TAYLOR, R S Measuring the unmeasurable or can we get there from here In *Approaches to measuring library effectiveness* edited by A F Hershfield and M D Boone Syracuse University 1972

TELL, B V Auditing procedures for information retrieval systems *Proceedings of the 1965 Congress. International Federation for Documentation* Oct 1-16 1965. Spartan Books 1966, 119-124

THOMASON, G F Managerial work roles and relationships *Journal of management studies* October 1966, 270-288 and February 1967, 17-29

TOBIN, J C A study of library use studies *Information storage and retrieval* 10 (3-4) Mar-Apr 1974, 101-113

TOTTERDELL, B and Bird, Jean *The effective library* Library Association 1976

TRIANDIS, H C Attitude measurement In *Research methods in librarianship measurement and evaluation by Herbert Goldor University of Illinois Graduate School of Library Science* 1968, 25-32

TWEDT, D K Some practical applications of the 'heavy half' theory 10th Annual Conference. Advertising Research Foundation 1964

URQUHART, J A and Schofield, J L Measuring readers failure at the shelf *Journal of documentation* Dec 1971 27 (4) 273-286

VICKERY, B C *Information systems* Butterworths 1973

VICKERY, B C et al *Metals information in Britain* Aslib 1969

VOOS, H *Information needs in urban areas a summary of research methodology* Rutgers University Press 1969

WALDHART, Thomas J and Waldhart, Enid S *Communication research in library and information science: a bibliography on communication in the sciences, social sciences and technology* Libraries Unlimited 1975

WARD, P Layzell The evaluation of library services In *Studies in library management* edited by Brian Redfern Clive Bingley 1971

WESSEL, C J Criteria for evaluating technical library effectiveness *Aslib proceedings* November 1968 20 (11) 455-481

WESSEL, C J and Cohrssen, B A *Criteria for evaluating the effectiveness of library operations and services Phase I Literature search and state of the art* John I Thompson & Co 1967

WESSEL, C J et al *Criteria for evaluating the effectiveness of library operations and services Phase II Data gathering* John I Thompson & Co 1967

WESSEL, C J and Moore, K L *Criteria for evaluating the effectiveness of library operations and services Phase III* John I Thompson 1969 AD 682 758

WHITE, Martin Information for industry — the role of the information broker *Aslib proceedings* Feb 1980 32 (2) 82-6

WHITTON, D Information and the quantity surveyor Construction Industry Information Group *Bulletin* Jan 1972, 21-22

WHY British Builders bungle the job (Anonymous) *New Scientist* 25th May 1978, 523-528

WILKIN, Ann Some comments on the information broker and the technological gatekeeper *Aslib proceedings* Dec 1974, 477-484

WILKINSON, J W Specifying managements information needs *Cost and management* September/October 1974, 7-13

WILLIAMS, Martha E Annual review of information science and technology Knowledge Industry Publications 11, 12 & 13 1977-9

WILLS, Gordon and Christopher, Martin Cost benefit analysis of company information needs *Unesco bulletin for libraries* 1970 24 (1) 9-23

WILLS, G and Oldman, C *The beneficial library* Cranfield School of Management 1977

WILSON-DAVIS, K The centre for research on user studies *Aslib proceedings* February 1977 29 (2) 67-76

WOLEK, F W The engineer; his work and needs for information *Proceedings of the 1969 ASIS meeting* 471-476 Greenwood Publishing Co 1969

WOLFE, J N et al *Economics of technical information systems* Praeger Publishers 1974

WOOD, D N Use studies: a review of the literature from 1966 to 1970 *Aslib proceedings* 23 (1) Jan 1971 11-23

WOOD, D N and Hamilton, D R L *Information requirements of engineers* Library Association 1967

YORKE, D A *Marketing the library service* Library Association 1977

ZAIS, H W *Economic modelling an aid to the pricing of information services* ASIS 1976

ZIPF, G K *Human behaviour and the principle of least effort* Addison Wesley 1949

ZWEIZIG, D and Dervin, B Public library use, users and uses In *Advances in librarianship* edited by M J Voigt and M H Harris, Academic Press 1977

INDEX

Accessibility 62
Activity sampling 39
Adelson R M 44
Afanasev E V 121
Aguilar F J 23, 113, 118
Allen T 21, 61 et seq, 82, 86, 143, 144
Alsop K 95, 98
Andrus R R 114
Architects 95 et seq, 101 et seq
Armstrong C M 17
Atkin P 9
Attitudes 53, 64
Austin B M 118
Barr A 56
Benefit inversion 72
Benefit segmentation 26, 67
Bird J 54, 56
Bishop D 95, 98
Blagden J 51, 77, 78, 132
Bommer M 16
Bonn G 72
Bookstein A 43
Braybrooke D 111
Brech E F L 111
Brewer E 118
British Institute of Management 122
Brittain J M 35
Brookes B C 100, 101, 128
Brophy P 9
Bryant E C 27, 38, 52, 54, 78
Buckland M K 56, 65, 69
Bureau of Applied Social Research 9, 14, 27
Burnett A D 54
Burns T 118
Burr R L 24, 54
Calder N 94
Campbell J P 114, 115
Carey A 33
Carlson S 118
Catherwood F 24
Cawkell A E 87
Childers T 87
Christopher M 74
Civil Engineers 96 et seq, 101 et seq

Clapp V W 72
Clark P A 33
Cohrssen B A 9
Collection evaluation 72
Consumer surplus 82
Control group 34
Cooper W S 58
Coover R W 9
Copeman G 118
Cost benefit analysis 20, 47 et seq
Cost effectiveness 20
Cranfield Institute of Technology 57, 64, 146
Criteria 34
Critical incident 43
Cuadra C A 9
Customer orientation 22
Daily Mail 55
Davis D L 43
Davis R A 99
Decision making — impact of information 23
Dehlinger H E 99
Department of the Environment 95
Derbyshire County Libraries 73
Derwin B 32
Diaries 40 et seq
Dickson W J 33
Disch A 40, 94
Document delivery 69 et seq
Document exposure 74 et seq
Drake J 42
Driver M J 32, 59
Drucker P 17, 55
Dudley E 56
Durham University 72
EVPI 74
Elinson J 33
Elwen P D 58
Ely D P 9, 86
Engineers 93, 94
Ensor J 14
Evans E 9, 100
Expectations 56, 65
Expected value of perfect information 74
Exposure 74

159

Fabisoff S G 9, 86
Failure analysis 71
Farrar C H 97
Fayol H 111
Feedback 42
Fishbein M 65
Flanagan J L 43
Flowerdew A D J 47, 48, 52
Ford G 9, 51
Fores M 117
Frost M 48, 53, 77
Gerstberger P G 93
Glover I A 111, 116, 117
Goddard H C 16
Gomershall A 42
Goodell J S 40
Goodey J 95, 99, 101
Gralewska-Vickery A 94
Greater London Council 78, 91, 92 et seq
Greenberg B G 87
Griffith B C 9
Guba E G 13
Haley R I 26
Hall R M S 99
Hall R W 20
Hamburg M 72, 74, 75 et seq
Hamilton D 13
Haney R 88
Hanson C W 94
Harris M H 88
Harrison A J 53
Hatt F 16, 17, 18, 26, 85
Havelock R G 9, 18, 19, 31
Hawgood J 72, 73
Hawthorne effect 33
Heavy half 25
Hill R W 41
Hills J A 9
Hindle A 63
Holmes P L 9
Horne J H 118
Hunter N 9
Impact 105, 128, 142
Information broker 40
Institute for Operational Research 44
Interviews 37 et seq
Jordan R T 72
Judge P J 53

Kalton G 129
Keegan W J 119
Kelly J 119
King D W 14, 15, 18, 27, 38, 52, 54, 78, 84
Kingston Upon Hull Public Library 13
Kish L 38
Knight R 57
Kramer J 76, 77
Kranzberg M 25
Krevitt B I 9
Kuehl P G 25
Ladendorf J 44
Lancaster F W 17, 18, 22, 47, 69, 70, 76, 78
Lantz B 105
Layard R 48, 50
Layzell-Ward P 9, 43
Least effort principle 62
Leavitt T 21
Libraries — definition 27
Library Association 55
Likert scales 56, 65
Lindley D V 74
Line M 9, 27, 37, 40, 57, 63, 71
Liston D M 86
Lubans J 56
Lupton T 118
Magson M 76, 79
Malthouse R F W 97
Management 111 et seq
Managers 111 et seq
Management by objectives 13
Mann P 37
Marcus T A 50
Marginal cost pricing 51
Marginal rate of substitution 82
Market segments 25
Marschak J 49
Martyn J 44, 78
Mason D 76, 77
Masterson W A 39
Matthew K 95, 99, 101
Mattison B F 87
McAlpine A 61
McCafferty M 9
McDonough A M 51
McLellan A W 18
McLuhan M 7, 22

Meier R L 75
Melrose-Woodman J E 49, 124, 125
Menzel H 9, 84
Ministry of Public Building and Works 96
Mintzberg H 119, 121
Mock T J 32, 59
Monument L 97
Moriarty J H 56
Morley R 72
Morris W E M 73
Moore N 9
Moser C A 35, 129
Murdoch J W 86
Newton T 49
Noble P 9
Norman J M 44
North American Aviation 94
Objectives 13
Observation 39
Oldman C 26, 54, 57, 64 et seq, 69
Olsen H A 9
Operational research 43 et seq
Orr R 16, 31, 37, 40, 43, 69, 94, 108, 144
Overheads 49
Palmour V E 14, 15, 18, 84
Panels 40 et seq, 67
Pareto 25, 70
Participant observation 39
Penetration 100, 123, 141
Performance appraisal 23, 114 et seq
Performance criteria 34
Personnel managers 125, 127
Politz A 76
Posdcorb 111
Pricing 47, 82
Principle of least effort 62
Product information 98
Product orientation 22
Quantity Surveyors 97, 101 et seq
Quarmby D J M 53
Questionnaires 37 et seq
Radner R 49
Rappaport A 114
Rees A M 58

Reinvention of the wheel 14
Relevance 57
Reliability 34
Remmers Kelly scale 56
Revill D 145
Reynolds R 9
Richardson S A 37
Ritchie E 63
Roberts M 95
Robertson A 41
Robertson S 100
Rodwell J 9
Roethlisberger F J 33
Rosenberg K C 76, 77
Rosenbloom R S 87, 123
Sampling 35
Sampling: systematic 129
Samuelson K 22
Saracevic T 59, 85
Satisficing 116
Schofield J L 71
Schrenk L P 45
Schulz D G 58
Score 83
Scout 83
Segmentation — marketing 25
Sequential interviews 38
Service components reliability and efficiency analysis 83
Service components utility analysis 83
Shadow pricing 82
Short E C A 9
Silvey R 25
Smith H A 41
Snow C 95
Solution development record 61
Stecher G 16, 54, 72
Stevens R F 97
Stewart R 117, 119, 120
Stock evaluation 72
Structural engineers 97, 101 et seq
Stufflebeam D S 13
Suchman E 33, 34, 87, 88
Sutton J R 99
Swanson R 31, 34, 39, 43, 77, 79
Sweeney G P 112
Systematic sampling 129

Tape recorders 41
Taylor P J 9
Technological gatekeepers 63
Telephone interviews 37 et seq
Tell B V 58
Terminal readers 16
Thomason G F 120, 121
Time saved justification 52 et seq, 76 et seq, 80
Time spent reading 20, 21, 118, 119, 120, 131
Tipton L 88
Tomlinson J W C 118
Totterdell B 54, 56
Trade literature 82, 98
Transfer pricing 49
Triandis H C 56
Twedt D K 25
Urquhart J A 71
Use 27, 53
Users 25
Utiles 58, 59
Utility analysis 82, 83
Validity 34
Value 20

Variables 31 et seq
Vickery B C 18, 20, 22, 31, 35, 44, 47, 78, 93, 116, 123
Voos H 55, 76
Waldhart E S 9
Waldhart T J 9
Ward, Layzell P 9, 43
Wessell C J 9, 54, 83
White M 40
Whitehead C M E 47, 48, 52
Wilkin A 40
Wilkinson J W 113
Williams M E 9
Wills G 26, 54, 65, 74
Wilson-Davis K 26
Wolek F W 87, 94, 123
Wolfe J N 47, 48, 49, 80 et seq, 99
Wood D N 9
Work study 39
Yorke D A 42
Zais H W 50, 51
Zipf G K 62
Zweizig D 32

SOUTHEASTERN MASSACHUSETTS UNIVERSITY
Z678.85.B12
Do we really need libraries?

3 2922 00057 359 9